When Writers Drive
the Workshop

When Writers Drive the Workshop

Honoring Young Voices and Bold Choices

BRIAN KISSEL

Foreword by
Aimee Buckner

Stenhouse Publishers
Portland, Maine

Stenhouse Publishers
www.stenhouse.com

Library of Congress Cataloging-in-Publication Data

Names: Kissel, Brian, author.
Title: When writers drive the workshop : honoring young voices and bold choices, K-5 / Brian Kissel.
Description: Portland, Maine : Stenhouse Publishers, [2017] | Includes bibliographical references and index.
Identifiers: LCCN 2016040682 (print) | LCCN 2017000519 (ebook) | ISBN 9781625310736 (pbk. : alk. paper) | ISBN 9781625310743 (ebook)
Subjects: LCSH: English language--Composition and exercises--Study and teaching (Elementary) | Writers' workshops.
Classification: LCC LB1576 .K495 2017 (print) | LCC LB1576 (ebook) | DDC 372.62/3--dc23
LC record available at https://lccn.loc.gov/2016040682

Cover and interior design by Lucian Burg, LU Design Studios, Portland, ME
www.ludesignstudios.com

Manufactured in the United States of America

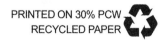

PRINTED ON 30% PCW
RECYCLED PAPER

25 24 23 22 21 20 19   9 8 7 6 5 4 3 2

During my first year of teaching, a second-grade spitfire named Tameka Allen entered my classroom and, ignoring my misguided prompts, wrote fascinating stories about her life. Her young voice was strong, and her bold choices in topics exposed me to a world quite different from my own. I consider her my most important teacher. She taught me that writers must drive the workshop.

Tameka must be nearing thirty now, and I have no idea where life took her after she left my classroom. But I hope her life is full—and I hope she's still passionately moving a pencil across a page.

I dedicate this book to her.

Contents

Acknowledgments

This book has been swimming in my head for more than twenty years now. When I was in the thick of teaching in my own classroom of young ones, I was too exhausted to commit my experiences to the page. And in my years as a professor, I had to go to others' classrooms to see possibilities I didn't know existed. I gathered the collected stories contained within this book from twenty years of valuable lessons I learned from teachers and students along the way.

I begin by thanking Joy Warner, a former classroom teacher who, along with her teaching colleague Leslie Tomko, had a bold vision to start a new school with a truly child-centered curriculum. Years ago, Joy invited me to the Community School of Davidson in Davidson, North Carolina, and allowed me to learn from brilliant teachers and their students. So many teachers at the school invited me into their classrooms to observe, teach, and share stories that I cannot possibly list all their names here. But I do want to acknowledge three teachers who allowed me to spend two years in their classrooms: Diana Hosse, Libby Christian, and Mary Mayo. I wish every student had an opportunity to learn from these three remarkable teachers.

I am grateful for Tisha Greene and Anne Lee, who allowed me to spend time with their teachers at Hidden Valley Elementary School in Charlotte, North Carolina. As a principal, Dr. Greene understands the importance of young children sharing their lives through writing. And Ms. Lee, a literacy coach, understands the important role teachers play in this process. They are committed, dedicated educators, and I am thankful to know them.

The most influential person in my professional life is my mentor and friend Jane Hansen. As a doctoral student at the University of Virginia, Jane taught me, "When you step into the professoriate, keep one foot firmly rooted in real classrooms." Since becoming a professor in 2006, I have spent one or two days a week teaching in K–5 classrooms. Jane's advice has kept me grounded and relevant. To date, it's the single best piece of professional advice I've ever received.

As a student at UVA, I was part of a teacher-research team led by Jane. It was modeled after the one she and Donald Graves started as professors at the University of New Hampshire. A group of us met weekly and talked about writing. Through the years, many folks weaved in and out of the group. I learned the most from these fellow researchers and friends: Jody Lawrence, Dorothy Suskind, Holly Tower, Kateri Thunder, Penny Bowles, Marianne Baker, and Robyn Davis.

I wish to thank two colleagues at the University of North Carolina at Charlotte: Karen Wood and Erin Miller. Karen has been a mentor, colleague, and friend—one of my biggest cheerleaders and someone with a generous heart. She constantly encourages and supports me. Erin read early pieces of this manuscript and gave me thoughtful feedback. I serve as Erin's mentor at UNCC, but she's such a wise soul that the roles should probably be reversed.

I must thank Tori Bachman, my glorious editor, who supported the development of this book and gave thoughtful feedback on every chapter. It's a gift to have someone in your life with a keen editing eye—an even greater gift when that same person has a hilarious sense of humor. Writing this book was hard work made much easier by sarcastic texts and e-mails she sent my way. You can thank Tori that you didn't have to read a comparison of high-stakes assessments to Burmese pythons invading the Everglades.

Finally, I wish to thank my family. Hattie, my wife, made breakfast in the morning and got the kids ready for school so I could sneak upstairs to write during the hours I was most awake. And in the evenings, when she was exhausted from teaching, she read every word of this book and gave me feedback from a teacher's perspective. Her insights made this a better book. She's a smart, gorgeous woman who is also my best friend. My parents always said I "married up." I spent the better part of my adolescence and young adulthood telling my parents they were wrong about everything... but, boy, were they right about this one!

I have three young children: Charlie, Ben, and Harriet. They are funny and charming and, frankly, sometimes a little naughty—they are my children, after all. They are also the reason I write. Hattie and I hope we are helping them live lives worth writing about.

Foreword

Once upon a time, not so very long ago, a man named Don Graves told us to listen to the children. Teach the writer. Live the way writers do. Do these things and you will nurture young writers beyond the assignment, beyond the curriculum, and beyond the schoolyear.

And so we did. Writer's workshop emerged as a prominent feature of the literacy landscape, with literacy leaders sharing their stories through books and conferences while teachers across the country worked hard to emulate them. Often I found myself bemoaning the fact that there was not a teacher's edition for the writer's workshop. I begrudged the many trips to the library to find my own resources, never being sure I was teaching the exact right thing. I wrote *with* my students. I wrote *for* my students. And I wrote *about* my students. And it worked. It wasn't magic; it was hard work. I talked with my students, I studied their work, and, with my curriculum in mind, I taught them. I taught them to be writers.

Today we are inundated with workshop resources. We have Pinterest, blogs, and websites with cute anchor charts, clever teaching tips, and prompts to go around. Today, we have published units that focus on using the workshop structure—teacher's editions!—complete with a teacher's modeled writing so you don't have to do your own if you don't like to write. We have rubrics and assessments and checklists to make sure every standard is met. We live in a world with so many workshop resources that we, the teachers, do not have to think much about it at all if we choose not to. With standards, assessments, and data, we have enough tools to drive our instruction so that if what we teach doesn't raise test scores, it's not our fault. It's a no-risk workshop. But . . . is that truly writer's workshop?

When Writers Drive the Workshop takes us back to the heart of Don Graves's work, while nudging us into the digital world we live in today. Brian Kissel reminds us that it isn't the standards, the assessments, or even the data that should be the major force driving our writing instruction. It's students. In order to teach the writer, not the writing, you need to focus on the writer—the human child—in front of you.

This book isn't really about fighting the way things are in education. It's about refocusing our attention during writer's workshop. It's a call to refocus on the student, the writer in front of us.

Starting with the very organization of this book, Brian puts students front and center. Most workshop books begin with the mini-lesson and work their way through the workshop parts chapter by chapter. But Brian, true to his message, starts with conferring—the heart of the workshop and the core of our teaching. Conferring is where the rubber meets the road and all of our teaching powers are zoomed in on one student. Brian reminds us to be quiet, listen, and then respond. Conferences aren't about checking off another standard but about teaching the writer to write well not only today, but also the next day, and the day after that.

After reconceptualizing conferring, Brian dusts off the author's chair and shines it like new. I love the way he invites his readers to look at the author's chair as a time for students to get the kind of response they feel they need. It's not a share and clap time, but rather a time for the community to come together, to rally around one writer's struggle or celebration, and to support that writer through his or her work with insightful suggestions and comments. This kind of reflective work—on the part of the writer, the student community, and the teacher—makes my heart sing! It is a simple twist on an old idea that not only works but also pushes us to empower students to take ownership of their writing.

Although *this* is a book that takes us on a journey to reclaim what we know is true about writing instruction and the way workshop should go, it also surges ahead into the twenty first century. With every chapter, Brian suggests ways to use technology to support the work we're doing in our writer's workshop. When reading professional development books, I usually cringe and skip over the technology aspects. They always seem too hard, too complicated, or too abstract for me to easily implement. But in these chapters, the suggestions seem doable and reasonable. I've tried several of his ideas now, and they work!

When Writers Drive the Workshop is written with the idea that we need to empower each student to lead the way on his or her journey of becoming a writer. Brian reminds us that listening to our students, not just analyzing data, leads us to the next teaching step. He reminds us that students are capable of setting goals and of reflecting on their own learning. What's more, this book is empowering to me, the teacher. The weight of standards, assessment, and data-driven teaching has sometimes blinded me to the children in front of me. This book, and this author, have reminded me that I have my priorities out of whack and that it's time to reset: students first; standards, assessment, and data second.

In a time in which we are inundated with resources to teach writing, this book stands out. Like a gentle wave, it pulls us back to remember what teaching in writer's workshop should be and pushes us forward to do the work well.

—Aimee Buckner
author of *Notebook Know-How*, *Nonfiction Notebooks*,
and *Notebook Connections*

Introduction

I   t has been more than thirty years since Donald Graves ([1983] 2003) first took us into classrooms of writers with his landmark book *Writing: Teachers and Children at Work*. In his book Graves describes how teachers and their students sat side by side and learned together as writers. Teachers brought their own writing experiences and know-how into the classroom to teach students and then listened carefully as children described their own decisions as writers. Teachers made instructional decisions based on their students' moves. What young writers said, and did, mattered.

For years, we've known that the structure of the writer's workshop (a mini-lesson, followed by a chunk of time for students to write and teachers to confer, culminating with an author's chair sharing experience) has been effective for young writers. But since the 1980s, writing instruction has shifted. We have entered an era of accountability in which results from standardized tests drive instructional decisions. Because of district-level mandates, many teachers think they have little choice but to toe the testing line, which often minimizes children's voices.

Today I'm worried. I'm worried because I know too many classrooms where mini-lessons begin with "seed" stories that germinate from laminated watermelons, predetermined conferences that always start with a compliment and end with a next step, and, if it's included at all, an author's chair or sharing time entirely driven by the teacher to reinforce a point he or she made during the mini-lesson. Rarely do children reflect on their writing. And if they do, it's often to fulfill a teaching agenda rather than a learner's agenda. When did packaged programs and Pinterest replace children as the driving force of instruction? When did everything start to look the same?

I'm in the midst of a midcareer reflection, looking back on my career as a teacher in pre-K through college classrooms but also looking forward to how we might be able to reenergize writing instruction. A quote from one of my favorite writers, Dr. Maya Angelou, often repeats in my mind: "Do the best you can until you know better. Then when you know better, do better."

In 1997, at the age of twenty-one, I graduated from my undergraduate elementary education program in New Orleans and accepted a job as a second-grade teacher in Jacksonville, Florida. In my undergraduate program I never had a class in teaching writing to K–5 students. I struggled in my first few months as a classroom teacher. I had been assigned a challenging group of students—maybe because I was the newbie, maybe because I was a man—and relied on scripted curricula, placed children in the same texts despite their disinterest, and chose the topics for their writing, all attempts to control the classroom and ultimately the students. I thought the road to knowledge had to be paved entirely by me. Boy, was I mistaken.

It soon became clear that I was floundering, so I began to educate myself. I went to workshops (one hosted by Lucy Calkins), read the work of writing researchers, and began to discover a path toward teaching that changed my instructional ways. Writing, more than any other subject, brought me into my students' lives. Story after story, memoir after memoir, informational text after informational text taught me new things about my students I *needed* to learn. And when I listened, I changed as a teacher. Here's the biggest lesson I learned:

To teach children, you must *know* them. To know them, they must reveal. To reveal, they must feel safe and secure. To feel safe and secure, they need agency. To have agency, they must have choices. When they choose their writing topics, children's lives unfold onto their pages. *We* are educated by the young voices and bold choices of our K–5 writers.

Like many teachers today who worry about teaching writing, I gave prompts for writing. I didn't listen much to my students. Conferring? I thought that was my time to grade the work piled up on my desk. When I did grade, I looked entirely at conventions, not meaning. I was proud when all the writing looked the same. I thought the goal was standardization, not individual expression. My lessons were prescribed—proudly ripped from the teacher's edition of a textbook telling me exactly *what* to teach and *when* to teach it. Jeez, I spent a couple of years as a lousy writing teacher. And the guilt of this instructional malpractice weighs on me still.

Over the last ten years I've spent two or three days a week in pre-K–5 classrooms during the time their teachers taught writing. I spent one day a week in classrooms where the students were mostly affluent, mostly white, and always fed. I spent another day in classrooms where the students were financially poor, entirely minority, often hungry, and aching to be treated with respect. One day I'd read children's writing about vacationing in grand hotels; the next day I'd read children's writing about living in run-down hotels. But no matter where the children came from, they all had one powerful shared need: they all wanted to be heard. And in this era in which tests have the loudest voices, isn't it about time for students to reclaim some voice for themselves?

In classrooms where I've spent time, I've wondered about these questions:

- What happens when students (not planned teaching points) lead writing conferences?
- What happens when students (not teachers) guide response at the author's chair?
- What happens when students (not tests) determine what they learn through reflection and self-evaluation?
- What happens when students (not prescribed curricula) lead the types of mini-lessons that need to be taught?
- Finally, what happens when teachers take all this knowledge from reflective learners and create the conditions—the physical and psychological spaces—in which students learn?

This book focuses on what happens when empowered *writers* direct the *writer's* workshop. In this book I tell *their* stories—those powerful stories that can come only from *authentic* classroom spaces where children are doing the important work of revealing their lives on the page. And, in telling their stories, I retell what I've learned in my teaching journey—a journey that is probably quite similar to yours.

In this book, we'll tour real classrooms where students set the writing agenda and drive with guidance from their teachers. We take this journey together across a familiar highway—the writer's workshop. Nancie Atwell (1998), Lucy Calkins (1994), Donald Graves ([1983] 2003), Ralph Fletcher and Joann Portalupi (2001), Regie Routman (2004), Jane Hansen ([1985] 2005), Katie Wood Ray (2001), and many other remarkable educators have laid the asphalt, painted the lines, and given us directions on how to travel this highway. I'm not interested in repaving those roads. Instead, this book focuses on what students have done and can do when given the opportunity to drive the workshop

—and what we can learn from the decisions they make as writers. It's about how these young voices and their bold choices can help us find our way as their teachers.

This journey will unfold in five chapters:

Chapter 1–Conferring: Writers Take the Wheel

I begin this book focused on conferring because it's the most important interaction that takes place between writers and their teachers. When we talk with students, they instruct *us*. Many teachers are hesitant about this aspect of the workshop for varied reasons: fear of the unknown, discomfort about what should be talked about, and uneasiness with facilitating individualized instruction within a whole classroom of writers. But when we listen intently to students, ask questions about their writing, and learn about them as writers, we are doing the important work of helping writers become self-reflective. In this chapter we listen in on various K–5 conferring sessions. We hear what students say, what teachers say in return, and what they learn from each other as a result. When we confer, we need to allow writers to take the wheel and steer.

Chapter 2–The Author's Chair: Writers Navigate the Response

The author's chair within a writer's workshop is an opportunity for the young writer to set the response agenda—to tell the class, "This is what I need from you as readers." That response may, indeed, be in the form of a compliment. But it could also be a call for ideas, a plea for revision suggestions, a yearning for validation, and a need for connection. In an author's chair, one writer shares her work and asks the class to offer feedback. As the child shares, everyone learns. In this chapter, we learn how the author's chair is a space for learning, not just for the author but for the other students and the teacher as well.

Chapter 3–Reflection: Writers Ponder the Journey

When we give writers the opportunity to reflect on their learning, we see a record of what our students value as learners. When writers reflect, they are able to name their learning, examine how they meet their writing goals, and set future expectations for themselves. In this chapter, I show ways in which writers self-evaluate through reflection. When they are given voice in this process, a more complete picture of their learning emerges.

Chapter 4–Mini-Lessons: Writers Determine the Detours

When writers drive the workshop, our instructional decisions depend on the trails they blaze with their writing. Too often, we create these trails for our writers by planning lessons before we know their strengths and needs. We've forged a path of instruction too rigid to allow the detours our students need us to make. In this chapter, we learn how to allow our students, not packaged curricula, to guide our instructional decisions.

Chapter 5–Conditions: Teachers Create Smooth Writing Experiences

Writers write with passion when teachers create conditions for smooth driving. Writers need *time* to drive, *choice* in driving style and destination, supportive *response* that propels them forward, *demonstrations* of effective processes and products, high *expectations* from their teachers and for themselves, a *room structure* that creates safe physical and psychological spaces, and the opportunity to *self-evaluate* what they value about their learning. In this final chapter, we discover the important role we play in creating a classroom space where we are co-drivers of the curriculum with our young writers.

In Chapters 1–4, I focus on the components of the writer's workshop. I include snippets of stories from real classrooms and describe practical ways you might embed these components within your own classrooms. Each of these chapters contains a section of guiding beliefs—a list of belief statements I use to ground my teaching practice. I also include a section of frequently asked questions (FAQs) toward the end of these chapters. These are common questions teachers ask me in classes, at conferences, or when I do work in schools. Finally, I include a Digital Diversion in Chapters 1–4 to help you see possibilities for using digital tools within your classroom.

Chapter 5, which focuses on the conditions teachers create, does not contain these sidebars because it offers a more holistic view of writer's workshop rather than an in-depth discussion of workshop components. Chapter 5 revisits the important foundational work of Donald Graves and offers in-depth descriptions of how teachers have embedded his conditions within their classrooms.

Allowing our students to control the decision making can be scary. I remember when I was a student driver in high school. I was fifteen years old, driving a stick-shift Subaru station wagon, and my mother was a wreck sitting next to me. Every couple of minutes she would throw her hands up on the dashboard—thinking her skinny arms would somehow stop an impending collision. Or she would vigorously pump the imaginary brake on her passenger side, hoping, somehow, that the force of her foot would stop the car. Over time, as I got better, her anxiety eased and she began to trust my ability to drive. I've seen this happen in classrooms as teachers give more choice and voice to young writers; their nerves ease as they see their students making good decisions and learning to trust their instincts.

Together now, we'll observe as students drive us around the workshop. Occasionally we'll give directions, pump the brakes, and change the radio station. Mostly, I hope we'll be able to just enjoy the ride together and reflect on how fortunate we are to be in the car with such interesting drivers, exploring an open road, taking in unexpected sights on an occasional detour, and learning along the way.

Chapter 1

Conferring: Writers Take the Wheel

*O*n a Monday evening, in my graduate-level course focused on teaching K–5 writers, my students and I immersed ourselves in a writer's workshop experience. It was our writing ritual—after settling into class, I conducted a mini-lesson, the class wrote, and we ended with an author's chair and reflection. On this evening, we focused on conferring. After writing together for a while, we met with a partner and conferred about our writing. Then we would discuss what happened during our conferences.

I wrote about my Grandma Kissel. She was a powerful figure in my life, and I chose to focus my piece on my last visit with her. I wrote about how she physically changed over time as the cancer crept from her colon to her brain—like kudzu overtaking a grand oak. I wrote about the weekend and how we spent it listening to stories from her youth. How she didn't want to stop hugging us when it was time to leave. And I wrote about how she stood on the porch as our car pulled away, waving desperately as tears poured down our faces.

When I finished reading the piece, I was upset. I had never written about this experience before, and I felt emotionally exhausted. But it was time for my partner to respond. And her response shocked me.

"Okay," she began robotically. "We always begin our conferences with a compliment, so I wanted to say that I think you included some really beautiful details. I really loved the descriptions about your grandma."

A compliment? I was taken aback. I wasn't really looking for a compliment. I was looking for an authentic human response. Maybe a tear. Maybe a sigh. Anything that felt honest:

"Wow, that really moved me" or "Gosh, what a tough memory that must be!" Instead, her well-intentioned response just felt hollow.

"Why did you decide to offer a compliment first?" I questioned.

"Well, that's the way I was trained to do a conference," she replied. "First a compliment, then a teaching point, then you give next steps, then the student heads off to fix his or her work." She described a conference the way I direct a sandwich artist at Subway—ham on wheat, white cheddar, lettuce, tomatoes, pickles. Just a little bit of mayo, red wine vinegar, no oil. Salt and pepper. Done.

This is what happens when teachers, not students, drive a conference.

I've worked with many teachers who say they've been told to adopt a similar, rote routine. This has always bothered me. As other aspects of the literacy curriculum grow more standardized, I worry that conferring might become another victim. We need to view conferences in less prescribed, rigid ways.

When conferring becomes the teaching act of making declarative statements rather than asking questions—a sermon rather than a conversation—where are our students' voices? If conferring is just the recitation of a predetermined set of teaching points, how do writers drive the curriculum? They don't. They become passengers in the backseat of a car being driven down a highway where agency and self-reflection are billboards that barely catch their attention.

Guiding Beliefs About Conferring with Writers

1. Listening is an act of instructional love.

One of my favorite shows on NPR is a series titled *Listening Is an Act of Love*, a project created by StoryCorps. There are interview booths throughout the country where two people can sit and interview each other. In the midst of the interview, we learn how the two are connected, and quite often, one person learns something about a loved one they never knew. To me, this is what a conference is: the instructional act of listening. As the conversation unfolds, both the teacher and the student learn. When we listen to our students, lessons unfold. The writer teaches the teacher, the teacher brings the lesson forward to the class, and the writing space becomes something that is co-constructed.

2. *Conferring is the act of asking rather than telling.*

There are four types of sentences: declarative (statements), interrogative (questions), exclamatory (conveying strong emotion), and imperative (commands). If, during a conference with a writer, I make more declarative and imperative statements than interrogative and exclamatory ones, I'm doing something wrong. A conference is not about me lecturing on what I already know; it's about encouraging writers to think and articulate their writing agendas. Telling enables; asking empowers.

3. *Conferring requires writers to set the conversational agenda.*

In our haste to save time, we too often bulldoze our way into a conference with a predetermined agenda. We do writers no favors by setting the agenda for them. I want writers to be self-reflective risk-takers. That means I want them to set the agenda, and I'll help keep the conversation flowing.

4. *Writers need authentic, human responses to their writing.*

In the movie *A League of Their Own,* the character played by Tom Hanks, in response to a baseball player who's crying, yells at her, "There's no crying in baseball!" Well, I don't think we can say the same for writing. If our children are truly writing based on their own writing agendas, they are writing in ways that provoke, inform, persuade, anger, scare, and make us laugh. And, yes, make us cry. Writers need us, as readers, to respond authentically to their work. It's the only way to show young writers how they are connecting with their readers.

Conferring in the Midst of Creation

In my first years of teaching, I missed opportunities to learn *about* and *from* young writers. Instead of conferring while students wrote, I chose to organize my desk or prepare the next lesson. I saw students' writing time as my get-other-work-done time. I suppose I never considered my important role in supporting children as writers. When I reflect on the choices my younger self made, I know why I avoided conferring: I didn't write much myself and never read with a writer's eye.

At a critical time in my young teaching life, I leaned on two important professional texts to build my conferring toolbox: *A Fresh Look at Writing* (1994) by Donald Graves and *How's It Going?* (2000) by Carl Anderson. Graves taught me to listen to the writer, ask questions, and learn about the writer beyond the classroom walls. Anderson taught me how to record conversations for analysis and how to manage my classroom so conferring could take place.

Next, I began writing. When I brought students to memoir writing, I wrote memoirs myself. When I taught informational how-tos, I crafted my own instructional manuals. As students composed poems, I wrote my own collection. When students sought to change the world with their persuasive pieces, I tried to do the same in my letters to politicians. As I immersed myself in writing, I learned the excitement of topic possibilities, the usefulness of making a plan, the struggle of revision, the minutiae of editing, the complication of publishing, the thrill of connecting emotionally with an audience, the satisfaction of turning an idea into a permanent something that would outlive me. In becoming a writer myself, I learned just how difficult, but satisfying, this process can be.

Most important, I talked with students. Instead of approaching students with fear about not knowing what to discuss, I approached them with the promise of open-ended possibilities. Instead of thinking, *I need to teach this student something profound*, I began thinking, *I need to listen to this writer and see what I can learn*. I needed to hear their voices.

In short weekly moments, I wedged myself between a writer and his or her writing. I observed, read, and asked questions. Then I listened carefully as the writer described his or her decisions while in the midst of creation. The voices of young writers teach us the tools we need to use when we sit to confer.

Conferring as a Conversational Act

I now realize my parents prepared me best to confer with writers. I grew up in that traditional nuclear family in which we sat at the dinner table each evening and engaged in conversations. We had a round dinner table, large enough for the five of us to have our own space but small enough to see the facial expressions that accompanied our words. From the sympathetic smile to the goading eye roll, the Kissel family dinner was either a nightly invitation to a comedy show or a provocation to a fight.

Around this dinner table we laughed ("Look what my face looks like with these grapes in my upper gums!"), cried ("You just don't understand me at all!"), debated ("Bill Clinton or George Bush?"), worried ("I'm nervous about my math test tomorrow"), informed ("Did you know starfish regenerate?"), pleaded ("But Bridget's parents are letting her go to the Ziggy Marley concert, and you know how strict they are!"), disciplined ("If you're going to eat with your elbows on the table, you'll eat off the floor with the dogs"), and dreamed ("Think I'm good enough to be a professional basketball player one day?").

My parents believed in the art of conversation. And to get good at conversing, you have to engage in it. You have to ask questions, look the person in the eye, connect, and be interested in what is said. You have to do two important things: *listen* and *respond*.

I worry we're losing this art form. How often do you go to a restaurant only to see faces buried in connected devices rather than people connecting with one another? Or, how often do you engage in a conversation with another person but find it's a one-way conversation? You ask questions about that person, but he or she never reciprocates by asking questions about you.

We have a social network of "friends" who may know us on a surface level but don't know us on deeper levels because they don't ask any questions. It makes you wonder, *Do they care?*

Do you think the students in our classrooms feel the same way? Maybe we know our students as learners on a surface level—as data points from some cold assessment—but don't know much about them off the page. Maybe we don't know the important information we need to know about their lives outside the classroom—the kind of information that coalesces to form a rounder, more robust, deeper understanding of them as human beings. Conferring is our way inside. When we confer, we're making listening an instructional priority. When we confer, we honor students' voices and learn about their writing choices.

In meaningful, important ways conferring allows us to

- **connect:** *In what ways do we personally connect with this writer?*
- **set goals:** *What goals might the writer set for himself or herself? What goals do we think the writer should consider?*
- **validate:** *What solid moves did the writer make, and how can we affirm those decisions?*
- **encourage:** *Where is the writer feeling vulnerable, and what can we say to keep him or her moving forward?*
- **teach:** *What do we know that the writer doesn't know yet, and how can we convey that knowledge to support the writer's next moves?*
- **assess:** *What insights into the writer did we gain by conferring?*

Many teachers tell me that conferring makes them nervous. Their hesitation comes from varied and valid places: fear of the unknown, discomfort about what they should talk about, and uneasiness with facilitating individualized instruction within a whole classroom of writers. But when we listen deeply to students, ask questions about their writing, and learn about them as writers, we are doing the important work of helping writers become self-reflective.

I believe in routine but not rigidity. And the types of conferences we conduct with students can be as varied as the students themselves. When we confer with students, we should consider the following possibilities:

- **Formal versus informal conferences:** *Most conferences are one-on-one formal conversations. Doing them every day, consistently, allows us to see every writer once a week. And when we sit down face-to-face with one writer and delve into his or her work, we can have richer, more meaningful conversations. But sometimes, when writers spend writing time reading like writers, generating ideas for writing, considering audiences and purposes for their published work, or publishing, our conferences can be less formal. An informal conference may be just a quick check-in—brief feedback on a simple issue a writer wants to address. During weeks when we blend together informal and formal conferences, we can typically get to writers more than once.*

- **Short versus long conferences:** *Formal conferences tend to be lengthier—four to five minutes per writer. Informal conferences tend to be shorter—a flurry of one- to two-minute check-ins on their process. Conferences that take longer typically focus on goal setting, planning, revision, and reflection. Conferences that take shorter chunks of time usually involve ideas for writing, text feature possibilities, editing, and publication tips.*

- **Small-group conferences versus individual conferences:** *Sometimes, maybe once every two weeks, instead of conferring one-on-one, you might consider conducting small-group conferences. Think of these as guided writing sessions, conducted similarly to how you might conduct a guided reading session. During small-group conferences several writers grapple with a similar writing issue. Maybe they are struggling to get solid writing ideas or need guidance in organizing their draft in coherent ways. Maybe they need to learn how to vary their sentences or develop characters in more three-dimensional ways. Or maybe it's a group of students who are finished with their writing and just want peers to respond to their published pieces. When analyzing conference notes, look for writers you can put together. These small groups share common writing interests or needs.*

Conferring does not need to fit some sort of one-size-fits-all structure. Writers need flexibility and variety in the ways we conduct our conferences.

Questions, Questions, Questions

Ultimately our goal as writing teachers is to confer ourselves out of a job. That is, we should try to take an instructional stance in which conferences serve as models for children to self-question. When we ask questions as we confer, we provide a model for students to self-question while we're off conferring with others—or when our writers have long left the classroom. When we begin to see writers asking themselves questions while composing texts, we know we're doing something right in conferences.

Important questions to ask include the following:

- "Who is your audience? What is your purpose?"
- "How might I help?"
- "What kind of conference do you want to have?"

Who Is Your Audience? What Is Your Purpose?

My favorite conferring questions focus on asking students about audience and purpose, because essentially, the questions get at the heart of *why* writers write. When we start with these two questions, we communicate to writers that their writing is supposed to go out of the classroom and into the world. Consider the following conference with a kindergarten student:

Brian: Hi, Ben. How ya doin' today?

Ben: Good.

Brian: What are you working on?

Ben: A book about trains.

Brian: Who are you writing it for?

Ben: Huh?

Brian: Who are you writing this book for?

[*Ben shrugs.*]

Brian: Have you ever thought of writing a book for someone else?

Ben: Nope.

Brian: Well, if you were going to write this book for someone, who would be interested in trains?

Ben: Hmm . . . I guess some of my friends.

Brian: Which friends?

Ben: Maybe Sam?

Brian: Why Sam?

Ben: Well, we play trains together all the time.

Brian: So, you think he might be interested in a book about trains?

Ben: Yeah, I think so. *[Shouting across the room to Sam.]* Hey, Sam. Want to read a book about trains that I'm writing?

Sam, *shouting back*: Sure!

Brian: Well, I think you found your audience.

Too often when I ask these questions, children respond in one of two ways: "I'm writing this for you [the teacher]" or "I'm writing this to get a good grade." But I'm not interested in writers *doing school*—fulfilling someone else's agenda. I'm interested in writers writing to entertain friends, inform peers, persuade parents, change minds, provoke tears, and project thinking. Because the author must be the one to determine the topic, audience, and purpose, consider setting the following rule for *all* students: *You must write for an audience other than me, and you must write for a purpose other than getting a grade.* When this rule is followed, the conversations that unfold illuminate meaningful purposes for their words.

How Might I Help?

Zoey, a fourth grader, pleaded as I began one workshop, "When it's time for conferences, will you please meet with me?" After a mini-lesson about character development, I found Zoey sitting at a small table, scraps of her story strewn across the top: three pages of continuous text, a scrap of paper with a new beginning, a scrap of paper with a different ending, and two scraps of paper with details from the story she forgot to add the first time around.

> Brian: What's going on today?
>
> Zoey: Oh gosh. My memoir is all over the place.
>
> Brian, *looking at all the scraps*: Yeah. Okay. I see lots of paper here. How can I help?
>
> Zoey: Well, I need to put it all back together again. I need help getting all this back in order.
>
> Brian: Sounds like you're revising, yes?
>
> Zoey: Yep. I have my main story here [*points at the three pages*], a different beginning here [*points at a scrap*], a different ending here [*points to a different scrap*], and some other parts I need to put in over here.
>
> Brian: So, when a writer revises, she adds, cuts, and rearranges, right?
>
> Zoey: Yeah. That's what I did here.
>
> Brian: Okay, what if you reread your story? Whenever there's a new part to the story, I'll cut the chunk. Then we'll see what we need to add, what can be cut, and how we can rearrange.

Zoey begins to reread her story aloud. As she reads, and with her permission, I cut her story into chunks. By the end of her reading, Zoey has twelve chunks of text dispersed in front of her. The conference continues.

> Brian: What do you think you should do here?

Zoey: I need to put all these in order first.

Brian: Yes! Then what?

Zoey: I need to see what parts need more details.

Brian: What parts usually need more details?

Zoey: The important ones.

Brian: Yep. Whenever I want a reader to linger on a moment or event, I slow it down by writing more about it. Okay, then what?

Zoey: Then I need to go back through and get rid of the stuff that doesn't matter.

Brian: Yes! Can you see any chunks that don't really add to the story?

Zoey, *pointing to a chunk*: Here.

Brian: Okay, that makes sense to me. What can you do now to help yourself get organized?

Zoey: I'm not really sure.

Brian, *writing on a sticky note*: Here are my suggestions: First, arrange all these chunks in order and number them. Next, glue each chunk on a separate page in your daybook [the teacher's term for a writer's notebook]. Ask yourself, *Which parts are important to keep? Which parts can I delete?* For each part you want to delete, put a line through it. Finally, decide which parts need a bit more detail. On that daybook page, add to the chunk. What do you think?

Zoey: Yep. I like it!

Imagine the same conference if I had barged in, set the agenda, given a teaching point divorced from what Zoey wanted as a writer, and then left. In what ways would I have stifled her writing? If I had made instructional decisions about Zoey *before* giving her the opportunity to express her desired direction, I would have not only taken away her agency but silenced an already knowledgeable voice.

Because we want writers to be self-reflective, another favorite question is "How can I help you today as a writer?" Students' responses to this question tell what they need even if they don't say it directly:

- "I don't know" often means they have not yet developed a self-reflective stance as a writer. Sometimes this is developmental. This question is a tough one for K–1 writers to answer. Model it with your own writing and give students ways they can help you develop your writing. Eventually, most students have enough experiences seeing us model this to begin having a rudimentary understanding of how to answer this question within their own writing.

- "I'm not sure" is usually a response from less-confident writers. They don't want to reveal what they perceive as their deficiencies. Instead, they want you to name them. Try to resist. "I'm not sure" usually leads me to ask more questions such as "Well, where are you in your process? What is frustrating you?" Push the self-reflection.

- "I need help getting ideas" may indicate that the writer has not connected with a genre. You may need to spend the conference time helping the writer find a reason to write. To discover possibilities for informational texts, you might say, "Tell me what you like to do when you're outside of school." To find narrative topics, you might help the child develop a time line and plot out important events from his or her life to turn into memoirs. For fiction, you might do the same thing with a character the child imagines. For persuasive pieces you might ask, "What's something you would love to change about this school [home, community, or world]?"
- "I need help revising" tells us that a writer has a solid start and needs help with refinement. Ask questions such as "What do you think is missing?" "What does your reader not know enough about?" and "Is there a different way to start or end your piece?" to guide the writer.
- "I need help publishing" reveals that a writer is ready for a final edit, materials to put it all together, and an outlet to make sure the writing is read by the intended audience.

When we ask students "How can I help?," we empower. We teach them that they are the agents of change—and that we're here to support them.

What Kind of Conference Do You Want to Have?

Oftentimes, it helps to walk into a conference asking, "What kind of conference do you want to have?" This way, depending on where writers are in their process, they can direct the type of response they need. It's presumptuous to think all conferences are about *helping* the writer. Sometimes, a conference is just a place to *hear* the writer. Consider, for example, this snippet from a conference with Delonda, a third-grade writer:

Brian: So, Delonda, how were you hoping I could help you today?
Delonda: Oh, I'm not looking for any help. I just wanted to talk to you about my writing goals today.

Delonda directed me to a page in her daybook where she had listed a series of goals such as writing longer pieces, developing characters using dialogue, and bringing more sensory words into her descriptions. She wanted to show me how she had met those goals in her most recent piece of writing. I had assumed Delonda needed my help, but she set me straight. She had an agenda for our conference and wasn't shy about redirecting its focus.

Toward the beginning of the school year, teach writers about the types of conferences available to them. In general, they are divided into the following categories:

- **Goals Conferences:** *conferences in which writers set goals, monitor goals, and reflect on whether they've met their goals*
- **Process Conferences:** *conferences that get writers thinking (rehearsal/planning), get writers writing (drafting), and help writers re-see (revision)*
- **Genre Conferences:** *conferences that enrich a writer's knowledge about particular structures of a genre and text features associated with that genre*
- **Skills Conferences:** *conferences that help writers edit their work (focusing on usage, spelling, punctuation) before going public*
- **Publication Conferences:** *conferences in which writers determine publication formats and outlets*
- **Portfolio Conferences:** *conferences in which writers choose artifacts, reflect on them, and explain what they've learned as writers*

Writers choose when a particular conference is needed—and their needs usually correlate with where they are in their study of a particular genre. In her book *Study Driven* (2006), Katie Wood Ray provides teachers with an inquiry structure for genre study. Using inquiry as a teaching stance, Ray proposes that teachers and writers learn about genres *together* by (1) gathering representative texts, (2) setting the stage for the study—including discussing purposes and audiences for writing, (3) immersing themselves in reading, (4) closely studying texts with others, and (5) "writing under the influence." As students study texts, and eventually write within a genre, the conferring that happens between the teacher and student typically mirrors the instructional continuum. For example, at the beginning of a genre study, as students immerse themselves in texts, teachers often confer with them about goals and potential purposes and audiences for their writing. Later, as students *write under the influence* of mentor authors they studied, they confer with teachers about where they are in their process. Figure 1.1 illustrates how conferring and genre study might inform and unfold on a continuum of teaching and conferring.

As I've grown as a conferrer, six simple words top my list of favorites: *who, what, when, where, why,* and *how.* Whenever I enter a conference with trepidation, I use those six words to empower young voices. And it's their responses to those questions that help guide my way.

	WEEK 1	WEEK 2	WEEK 3	WEEK 4	WEEK 5	WEEK 6	WEEK 7	WEEK 8
Genre Study Focus	Immersion in Reading and Close Study of Genre Features	Planning and Rehearsing	Drafting Multiple Texts	Choosing One Draft for Publication	Revision	Revision	Editing and Publishing	Publishing and Celebration
Typical Type of Conference Requested by the Writer	Goals Conference	Process Conference Genre Conference	Process Conference Genre Conference	Process Conference Genre Conference	Process Conference Genre Conference	Process Conference Genre Conference	Skills Conference Publication Conference	Publication Conference Portfolio Conference

Figure 1.1 A Conferring Continuum

If questioning gives us insights into the writer's thinking, documenting those responses provides the data we need to analyze what they know and to set new learning goals with our writers. After asking questions, documenting their responses is the second-most important teaching act we do as conferrers.

Document, Document, Document: Making a Record of Our Writers' Voices

I'm father to three young children—twin boys in second grade and a daughter in first grade. They are only twenty-two months apart. I love them dearly, but they are responsible for a significant amount of memory loss. Sometimes, at my wife's request, I go downstairs to get a new roll of toilet paper and come back upstairs five minutes later with a magazine and a cheese stick. "Where's the toilet paper?" my wife will ask. Most often my response is, "Whoops. I forgot."

If I can't remember toilet paper, there is no way I'll remember a five-minute conference I had with a writer the week before. If I don't record, I don't remember.

Writers need responders who remember—and documentation provides much-needed memory space. We lose track of our writers' voices and their decision-making choices when we fail to document our conversations. Writers go unnoticed when we don't remember whether we met with them; they go unvoiced when we fail to meet with them weekly. And, writers' voices become unnecessarily repetitive when we fail to record notes from previous conversations—precious minutes wasted recalling

Digital Diversion: Digital Conference Notes

I'm usually a pencil-and-paper kind of note taker. When I confer, I grab a notebook and writing utensil. I tried taking digital notes, but I found myself spending too much time staring at a screen and not enough time looking at writers or their writing.

In my work with teachers, however, several swear by digital note taking. They say it's quicker and easier to organize, and makes finding patterns less labor-intensive. I believe them. Just as there's no one way to confer, there's no one way to take notes. If typing conference notes works for you, do it! What matters is that you're recording the conversations.

Here are two ways teachers have gone digital with their note taking:

- **Confer App:** *You know that saying, "There's an app for that!" Yes, there is an app for conferring that several teachers use in classrooms. Confer App (www. conferapp.com) was created by teacher David Lowe as part of a project he designed for his National Board Certification. The tool allows teachers to input conference notes about students' strengths, a teacher's teaching point, next steps, and student goals. Each student has his or her own folder, allowing teachers to easily recognize individual strengths and needs. But the app also allows teachers to find common needs and strengths, quickly helping them bring together small groups of students with similar needs.*

- **Evernote:** *Evernote is another popular tool teachers use to create and organize conference notes. Evernote allows teachers to keep a multimodal record of the conference that includes typed notes, photos of writing, and voice recordings. Teachers can create separate folders for each student, write conference notes, and tag them for organization. An excellent example of one teacher's use of Evernote can be found at the Two Writing Teachers website at https://twowritingteachers. wordpress.com/2013/08/18/evernote-mere/.*

what was already discussed. If we derive future lessons from our conversations with writers, we must have notes to analyze for planning. Documentation helps guide our instructional decision making. Students' voices resonate and are reflected in our instruction when we record snippets of what they say.

Document to Ensure You've Seen Everyone.

Because conferring is the most important part of our instructional time in the workshop, we need to see every student at least once a week—twice, if possible. Our conferring can't happen haphazardly. *Every* child needs response. And we are responsible for ensuring that such response happens consistently.

In my early years of teaching, I failed to keep a solid record. As a result, I gravitated toward one type of writer: those who required lots of scaffolding. I spent the majority of my conferring time with those I believed needed me the most.

Is this the case for you as well? Here's a five-minute quick-write exercise to see if you do the same:

- Take a piece of paper and divide it in half lengthwise.
- Quickly write the names of all the students on the left side.
- Now, set a five-minute timer.
- On the right side, jot down as much as you can possibly remember about them as writers (such as strengths, weaknesses, and types of things they write).
- When the timer goes off, stop.

Look at your list. What do you notice? Who did you write about first? Who was easy to write about? Who still has blank space next to their names?

Likely, those students you wrote about first are the writers you gravitate toward when conferring. You know them the best, and you probably had plenty to say about their writing ability. I predict they are probably your weaker writers. After all, doesn't it seem like administrators want us to constantly home in on deficiencies rather than strengths?

You probably also had plenty to say about those writers you believe are your stronger ones. You probably hold them up as exemplars in the class. They are probably the ones *everyone* knows is strong. Other students know this, too. That's why they are sought-after writing partners.

Now look at the blank spaces. Who are those you don't know well enough as writers? Those are your writers who write in the shadows—the ones who write without drawing much attention. Likely, they are just fine academically; you're not worried about their progress. They are your voiceless students. And they need to be heard.

Over the years I have experimented with several different ways to ensure I meet with all writers, many of which I learned from others. Here are three methods I have found to be most effective:

- **Class-at-a-Glance:** *Create a class-at-a-glance grid (Anderson 2000) in which you write the names of all your students in individual boxes, and then place the grid in a sheet protector. Each time you meet with a student, use a dry erase marker to check the name. Once all names are checked, erase the sheet protector and start over. See Figure 1.2 for a look inside how I organize my conference notebook.*
- **Mini-Notebooks:** *In her wonderful videos about conferring with readers, Debbie Miller (2002) explains how she uses individual mini–spiral notebooks to confer with readers. Each student has an individualized notebook that Debbie keeps in a container. When she goes to confer, Debbie pulls four or five mini-notebooks from the front of the container—those will be the students with whom she confers that day. At the end of the workshop, she places those notebooks in the back of the container. The next four or five will be chosen the next day. As she walks toward each child to confer, she flips back through her students' notebooks to read what happened at the last conference. What a brilliant strategy to carry over into writer's workshop!*

Inside Brian's Conference Notebook

To keep myself organized for conferring, I carry around a three-ring binder divided into two sections: one section includes my teaching tools for conferring, and another section contains documentation for each writer. Here's an explanation of my organization:

Section 1: Tools for Conferring

I create a binder for each genre study I teach. The binders contain copies of mentor texts (professional and student created), lesson plans, mini-lesson sheets, planning sheets, and anything else that serves as a teaching resource. Each time I begin a new genre study, I pull the resources from the genre binder and place them in my conference notebook. The first section of my conference notebook contains the following:

- **Alphabet/Sound Cards:** For younger children, I laminate miniature cards that contain the letters of the alphabet. They have both upper- and lowercase letters printed on them. Often, young children want me to help them sound out words or labels for their drawings. These cards, readily available, help me do that.

Figure 1.2 Inside Brian's conference notebook

- **Copies of Mentor Texts:** I like to keep photocopies or actual copies of mentor texts at the front of my conference notebook, because sometimes I pull them out to show a certain technique an author used in his or her book. I might want to show a beginning, an ending, or a way the author developed a character. This is why it's important for me to have readily available mentor texts to use when the occasion arises.

- **Copies of Student-Created Mentor Texts:** I photocopy texts written by former students to use from year to year. As students engage in their brainstorming-planning-revision-editing-publishing processes, I may take photos of the interesting ways in which they engage in these processes on paper. I'm also on the prowl for published pieces that I think are well developed, well organized, well structured, and clearly edited. I add these to binders I create for specific genres. Then, when it's time to teach this genre the following year, I have examples of student-created texts (that are grade-level appropriate) to share with students.

- **Mini-Lessons on Daybook Sheets:** Whenever possible, I like to summarize my mini-lessons on half sheets or quarter sheets of paper. I print these out and ask students to glue them into their daybooks. This way, students can carry these lessons around with them wherever they go. I sometimes think this is more effective than anchor charts because they are easier for children to access and see. When I print them, I always make extra copies and place them into a sheet protector. Then, when students need me to reteach a particular lesson during a conference, I have the lesson available to use from my conference notebook.

- **Conferring Questions:** Before I felt comfortable conferring, I had a list of conferring questions I used as a support. These questions are included in my notebook to remind me that my primary job is to ask questions during a conference.

- **Monthly Checklist:** I keep a monthly checklist of writers I confer with in a sheet protector. Then, after meeting each writer, I use a transparency marker and place a check mark in his or her box. At a quick glance, I can see who met with me and who I have yet to meet with that month.

Figure 1.2 Inside Brian's conference notebook (continued)

Section 2: Individual Writers

Section 2 of my conference notebook contains information about individual writers. In this section, every child in the class has his or her own tab, and I keep the following data for each writer:

- **Individual Goals Sheets:** At the beginning of each genre, I'll ask writers to set goals for themselves. I might ask, "What do you want to learn during this study? How are you hoping to grow as a writer in the next few weeks?" Students reflect and write goals for themselves. Then, throughout the study, we'll revisit those goals. I keep a copy of their goals sheets in my conference notebook so we can monitor progression toward their goals.
- **Individual Conference Sheets:** These are the sheets I use to record my individual conferences. I keep a sheet for each student so I can see monthly progress.
- **Assessment Data:** If there is a genre I'm teaching where I want to collect specific data, I'll include a checklist of those skills for each student. I'll assess their work in different ways, including (1) assessing their writing process, (2) assessing their habits as writers, (3) assessing their final products, and (4) asking them to self-assess. I keep records of these assessments under their individual tabs.

Figure 1.2 Inside Brian's conference notebook (continued)

- **Designated Conference Days:** *You might also experiment with designating specific conference days for writers so they know when you plan to confer with them. Each Monday, you can display a chart with student names listed under each day that week. Students plan their conferring agendas accordingly. They think ahead to what they want to discuss—another tool to empower writers to make decisions about what they want from a conference.*

Document to Discover Emerging Patterns.

It's not enough to just transcribe conversations. Take notes to discover patterns—patterns occurring within the individual writer and patterns occurring across the entire classroom of writers. Analyze these notes every two weeks, with a deeper analysis at the end of the month. When I analyze conference notes, I ask myself the following questions:

- *What are the strengths of this writer?*
- *What are the challenges this writer faces?*
- *Where do we need to go next?*
- *What can the whole class learn from this writer?*

Here's a peek inside a set of conference notes with Amir (see Figure 1.3), a fourth-grade student writing to persuade his teacher and principal that Minecraft is an educational tool that should be allowed in the classroom.

When we analyze Amir's conference notes, several strengths emerge. As a writer, Amir

- chooses a topic that is meaningful for him, a topic he feels passionately about as a writer;
- determines an appropriate audience for his writing (*teacher and principal—the decision makers who have power at the school*);

Name:	Amir			
Date:	2/3	2/9	2/16	2/23
Genre:	Opinion	Opinion	Opinion	Opinion
Type of Conference:	Planning	Revision - Adding	Revision - Clarity	Revision - Beginnings
What we Discussed:	· He has chosen topic (Minecraft) · Knows audience (teacher, principal) · Wants Minecraft in classroom. Says it can be teaching tool.	· He has drafted · Has 2 reasons to support his argument · creativity · math problem-solving · Wants more reasons · Needs the reasons for the counter argument.	· Having hard time finding supporting evidence on-line. · I taught the iSEARCH stratgy. · We found several websites to support both sides. He will go back in and add /revise.	· Struggling to begin in a way that convinces. That talked about: · surprising facts. · Description · Quotes "I want people to really consider changing this!" Amir
Strengths:	· Self-chosen topic · Clear audience · clear purpose	· Solid draft (1-2 pages + reasoning) · Clear passion for topic.	· Knows what he doesn't know!	· Understands the importance of hooking a reader.
Challenges:	· Knows his side clearly. Needs to figure out the other side of argument.	· Needs to do research of other side. · Stronger beginning/ ending	· Conducting searches on Internet.	· Beginning · Next → Ending!
Possible Mini-Lessons	Audience / Purpose	Articulating Reasons	iSEARCH strategies	Beginnings / Endings of Opinion Pieces

Figure 1.3 Amir's conference notes

- provides a real purpose for writing (*to enact change in the school*);
- articulates reasons why Minecraft is an educational digital tool;
- writes with passion; and
- writes a strong beginning that makes me want to keep reading.

We can also notice several challenges. Amir still needs to learn how to

- use examples and research to support his reasons;
- convince the audience using persuasive data;
- acknowledge counterarguments;
- conduct searches on the Internet that will elicit useful information; and
- critically evaluate sites to ensure he cites accurate information.

In subsequent conferences with Amir, you would provide reassurances—voicing strengths and reinforcing the solid moves he makes as a writer. You may not immediately know these strengths, so analyzing conference notes will guide you.

You may also notice challenges Amir faces as a writer. But don't name these challenges in the conference. Not yet. Instead, question. You want Amir to self-reflect and discover them on his own. The types of questions you ask will come from reviewing the conference notes.

It's also wise to maintain a month's worth of conference notes for each writer across one sheet of paper so you can look at student progression across several weeks of conferring. This allows you to skim across the page to see where you've been and where you need to go next in your conversations. It gives us a record of the writer's thinking—a record of the writer's voice over spans of time.

Document to Teach.

Individual conference notes provide an instructional vision for the whole class. I've worked with teachers who, during monthly planning meetings, just bring conference notes to the session. They share what their writers are doing (or not doing) and discover patterns across multiple students. Analysis of the conference notes tells them what needs to be taught next. What a productive use of planning time!

Often, upon conferring with students, you might discover an important mini-lesson that needs to be taught to the whole class because it's a recurring issue with many of them. For example, Amir was not the only one who needed help critically analyzing information found through web searches. As I conferred with others, I discovered that just about every student had difficulty navigating the overwhelming maze of search results. Reflection on conference notes reveals instructional next steps, providing us a road map for future lessons. (I write more about this road map in Chapter 4, which focuses on mini-lessons.)

Document to Assess.

In his book *Teaching Day by Day* (2004), Donald Graves writes, "We cannot wait for or expect people from out of town to assess our students—or trust them when they do. True assessment exists in the classroom; children need to know how to assess their own work" (169). When we document our conversations, we capture the rich language that writers wrap around their learning. It's a breathing document of writers' decision making. And it's an opportunity to document their voices in the assessment process.

Conference notes provide counternarratives to the testing data that fail to measure the complex, nuanced ways in which our learners are growing. I recall a fourth-grade student, a brilliant writer, who wrote freely and beautifully outside of an assessment setting. But as soon as the writing assessment started, he couldn't write. Instead of his pencil marking the page, tears soaked the page. He failed the assessment despite being one of the best writers in the classroom. How often do we have bright, capable readers and writers who score surprisingly poorly on assessments? How many times have we seen students freeze on these high-stakes tests because of the intense pressure being placed on them to score well? In this time of privatization and corporate takeover of education, the system seems set up for our children to fail. Actually, it's good for business if they do.

Frequently Asked Questions About Conferring

1. How do I confer with every student?
The most effective teachers I've seen have a consistent routine of meeting with four to five students a day, which allows them to see every student once a week. During weeks that are interrupted by holidays, days off, or special events, I've seen teachers do shorter, more focused conferences to meet with every child. It's important for us to touch base weekly with our students, even if we need to do quick check-ins.

2. What are all the other students doing while I'm conferring?
Writing. If they're not writing, you'll want to do a procedural lesson to remind students that writing time is precious—and shouldn't be wasted. You might also remind students of upcoming deadlines so they'll head back to work.

3. How do I deal with students who constantly interrupt me while I'm conferring with others?

Many teachers have a cueing system using props to remind students not to interrupt. You might wear a hat or another easy-to-see visual that lets students know you are in the midst of conferring and should not be interrupted—unless there's an emergency. Occasionally, I have to tell students, "How would you feel if I was distracted when I was trying to listen to you?" And sometimes, I'll simply keep my eyes on the writer and ignore the child trying to interrupt—or point the child back to his or her writing space.

4. What if I have a student who never sits and writes independently?

Every teacher has the class roamer. This student usually likes to roam to one end of the classroom to sharpen his pencil. Stroll to the other side to see what's happening outside. Check in on friends. Go to the bathroom. In one classroom, a teacher brought in laundry baskets for her second graders to sit in. She suggested her roamers use laundry baskets to create individual writing spaces. It was a perfect solution. Her students were better able to concentrate on their writing, and it eliminated all the unnecessary movements.

5. Don't I always need to begin a conference with a compliment?

No. I think you should find and acknowledge students' strengths. But I believe conferences should be conversations. And if you always follow a strict routine during response, it feels inauthentic to the writer.

When test scores tell one side of an uneven story, conference notes empower us to tell the other side. When we document our conferences, we're retaining the voices of our students—the ones who are often silenced when they become data points rather than human beings.

Travelogue

I end this chapter by reflecting on a conferring experience with Demetria, a second grader composing an informational text. She sits at her seat, eyes cast upward, pencil eraser in mouth as she ponders. Several pages of blank paper are stapled together, and she's not quite sure how to begin. When I sit next to her, we confer:

Brian: How ya doing today?

Demetria, *smiling widely*: Good!

Brian: What are you working on?

Demetria: Oh, I'm thinking about this book I want to write. It's all about hotels.

Brian: Looks like you're making a plan in your head, huh? Want to talk with me about it? Maybe I can help you plan.

Demetria: Sure!

Brian: So, you know a lot about hotels, huh? Do you like to stay in hotels a lot?

Demetria: Oh, I don't stay in hotels. I live in them!

Brian: I didn't know you lived in a hotel.

Demetria: Yep. I've lived in hotels for a while now. Well, I mean, we stayed at the Sunset Inn for a while. Then we moved to the Sleep Inn. Then we moved over to the motel. Then we stayed in the one across the street. You know that one?

Brian: No, I don't. Sorry! Want me to look it up?

Demetria: Nah. It don't matter. They all about the same. Well, anyway, we stayed in that one for a while. We kind of move around a lot. Kind of from one hotel to the other.

Brian: Wow. I didn't know that about you. I just learned something new! Well, you're working on this informational book about hotels. I wonder, have you thought about an audience for this book? Have you thought about who this book might be for?

Demetria: Well, you want to know about it?

Brian: Yes. Of course!

Demetria: Well, then, I write it for you.

Brian: I definitely want to learn more. But I'm sure there are others who might be interested. Can you think of other people who might be interested in this book?

Demetria: Maybe some kids in here might want to know more about it. I don't think there are others who live in hotels. I think they live in houses. Or maybe apartments. So, they might want to know. They don't know how much fun it is to live in hotels. I can tell them about it.

Brian: Fun? Okay, tell me more.

Demetria, *sounding excited*: Did you know hotels have TVs in them? And they have these machines. These big machines that if you can find some money on the ground, you can get yourself some Cheetos! Or some Snickers bars. Yep! That's right. And hotels have water! You just open up the sink in the bathroom and water comes pouring out. It's nice. Me and my brothers and sisters, we can run up and down the balcony. We play some hide-and-seek. Sometimes we jump back and forth from the beds. But then Mama gets mad at us, so we stop. Man, I just love living in hotels!

Brian: That does sound fun!

Demetria: Yep. It is! The only bad thing about the hotels is when people get in fights next door. Like, sometimes at night you can hear them fightin'.

Brian: Oh jeez. Is that scary?

Demetria: Sometimes. Mama just tells us to close our eyes and go back to sleep. We know it's okay, though. Because we can always just move to another hotel. That's another good thing about living in hotels. You can move whenever you want!

Brian: Wow. Well, that is a good thing, isn't it? When it gets a little scary, you can always move. Hmm . . . kind of reminds me of what happens when I write, actually. Sometimes I get a little scared about what I'm writing and what people are going to think about my writing. But I know that whenever I get scared, I just have to keep moving forward. I just have to keep writing.

Demetria: Yep.

Brian: I heard you say several great things about living in hotels. I wonder if each thing could be a separate page in your book. What do you think?

Demetria: Okay.

Brian: I'm thinking you could have your first page just describe where you live. Like, you said that many of your friends live in houses or apartments, so you might think about telling readers that some people live in hotels.

Demetria: Yep. Good idea!

Brian: What do you think you should do on the other pages?

Demetria: I can have a page about the TVs. And then I can have a page about the food machines. I can do a page about the water. I can do a page about playing games.

Brian: Yes! You could even end it like you described it to me. Talk about the scary part, but then how you have the freedom to move if it ever gets too scary. What do you think about that plan?

Demetria: Yep. I like it!

Brian: Okay, sounds like you have a plan.

Demetria: Yes!

I've long ago given up the idea that the sole purpose of conferring with children is for the adult teacher to impose wisdom downward onto young, novice writers. I've had too many conferring experiences in which I learn more about writing, and life, from the writer than the writer learns from me.

The privileged me—the one who comes from a childhood of financial stability where hotels were places we slept while on vacation—initially felt sorry for Demetria and upset about a child living in uncertainty. But then she talked, describing a world where simple pleasures—like a working television, running water, and vending machines—are magical extravagances. Something I take for granted, she celebrated.

What do we learn when we confer with children? Well, we learn about the decisions they make (or don't make) as writers. And this information, indeed, tells us our next instructional moves. But in the midst of conferring, I think we learn even more important information about our writers. We learn a bit more about why our children might need a nap in the middle of the day, why they might chow down at breakfast and still want an extra biscuit an hour later, and why they linger in the classroom even after they've been called for the bus home. We learn about the brother or sister who is sick or bothersome or favored. We learn about the glories of a great friendship or the burden of a friendship gone awry. We learn that they love trains, Legos, Minecraft, playing outside, dressing dolls, playing store, riding bikes, dancing, and Taylor Swift. We learn about the great joys and the horrible moments that define a life.

Demetria taught me a lesson about hope. She taught me what resilience looks like from the perspective of an eight-year-old. Where I might see an unpaved road of deep cracks and potholes, she taught me to look at the dandelions growing through. In her own way, she whispered, "When life gets scary, move onward." I learn many lessons when I'm open to learning as much from the writer as the writer learns from me. Conferring is not just a conversation about writing. It's a conversation between two human beings—both learning about writing. And that's what we discover when we allow writers to drive the conversation.

Chapter 2

The Author's Chair: Writers Navigate the Response

"*Okay, everyone, it's time to gather on the carpet for author's chair," I announce to my second graders.*

Students join me on the carpet. They bring their writing, sit to face the chair, and nervously wait to see which name I pull from the soup can of wooden craft sticks.

Thom's name is drawn from the can. A recent immigrant from Cambodia, Thom sits excitedly in the author's chair. He is in his second year in the United States, and his confidence as a second-language speaker and writer has grown.

Thom begins. His words fly out like the quick staccato beats of a drum. "Okay, guys. Here it is. Martin Luther King. Yep. I wrote about him today. Yep, I wrote about him yesterday, too. But I want to read it now. Here I go. You ready? You listening? Okay, here I go."

Thom begins to read:

Martin Luther King Had a Dream

"Martin Luther King Jr. is a nice guy and he was a great family. On this paper I'm going to tell you about Martin Luther King Jr. who had a dream. Martin Luther King Jr. had a dream about sharing stuff together. Martin Luther King Jr. dreamed of everyone wanted respect one another and he had a dream of every one will get along with each other.

"We should keep Martin Luther King Jr. dream alive by sharing stuffs. We should keep Mr. Luther King Jr. dream alive so people will share pencil and share some other stuff at school or somewhere else."

The class claps. Several hands rise in the air. "Thanks for sharing, Thom," I say. "Let's tell Thom what we like about his writing."

Sarah frantically waves her hand. "Sarah, go for it," I say.

Sarah responds, "I like Martin Luther King, too. That was good!"

"Thank you," Thom replies.

Another hand waves back and forth. "Okay. Sam, I see you raising your hand. What compliment can you give Thom?"

"I like Martin Luther King," Sam says. "I like his dream, too."

Thom offers the same curt reply. "Okay. Thanks."

"We have time for one more," I announce. "Tamara. What would you like to say?"

"I like that Martin Luther King shared stuff," Tamara offers. "That was nice of him."

Thom says, "Yeah. Me too."

Thom shared, the class responded, and the wooden craft stick moves from the "Yet to Share" can to the "Shared" can. The author's chair ends for the day.

Confession time. As a new classroom teacher, I ran a terrible author's chair. When I reflect on this scene, I notice the following:

- I chose the author who shared—from a can!
- I chose who responded to the author.
- I even chose the type of response they offered.

My author's chair lacked choices—and the lack of choices led to silenced voices. I didn't yet subscribe to the belief that authors are the "author"ities on their writing—and I certainly didn't consider that they could direct the audience response. Authors who sat in the chair in my classroom fulfilled an instructional agenda rather than an author-led one. Ugh. Missed opportunities!

My thinking about the author's chair changed one evening during a graduate class I took with Jane Hansen, who, along with Donald Graves, wrote the influential article "The Author's Chair" (Graves and Hansen 1983). That evening, before anyone shared a piece of writing, Jane asked a simple question: "How would you like for us to respond to your writing?" With that one small question, my thinking was transformed.

I never thought that maybe the author should have this choice. Many of us in Jane's class never considered empowering the author with choice because we never did such things in our own classrooms. We either told the audience how to respond to the author or allowed audience members to respond however they liked. We conducted teacher's chairs or audience chairs and stripped power from the person perched on the seat—vulnerable to whatever response emerged from the class.

When any author, young or old, sits in a chair and commands the attention of an audience, identity and agency coalesce. The writer sits and believes, *I am an author who has something to say; you are the readers who can offer responses to push me forward.* When we take the pedagogical stance that writers should be the reflective agents of their process, the author's chair becomes a powerful seat—one that requires thoughtful, practiced beliefs (Kissel, Miller, and Hansen 2013).

Guiding Beliefs About the Author's Chair

The following beliefs reveal my understanding of the author's chair. These beliefs guide my practice in classrooms and keep me focused on its purpose:

1. Authors in the author's chair are "author"ities on their writing.

All authors who sit in the chair know themselves as authors better than the people sitting in the audience. And if they don't (as is the case with many young or less confident writers), the author's chair gives them the experience to help develop this knowledge. Authors often know their strengths and struggles as writers. That makes them the "author"ities on their writing.

2. Authors in the author's chair decide the audience response.

When authors sit in the author's chair, they use their "author"itarian knowledge to direct our response. Authors tell us they need compliments when they want to know how they did as writers, questions when they want to see gaps in their writing, suggestions when they need to revise, connections when they want to know how their writing affects others, and ideas when they come to the chair with a blank page. They read their writing with a purpose, and the audience responds accordingly.

3. Authentic, respectful response informs the author at the author's chair.

Donald Graves (1994) wrote, "Writing is a social act. Writers write for audiences. Teachers work to provide a forum for authors to share their words, as well as to help their authors learn how to be good readers and listeners to the texts of others" (146). Audience members have an important role in the author's chair. They must listen—closely and carefully. And they must offer response to the vulnerable writer who has taken great personal risk to share his or her writing aloud. Teachers are responsible for teaching the types of responses that inform rather than hinder, strengthen rather than weaken the writing, and support rather than diminish the writer. Writers don't just share their writing in the author's chair—they share their lives. Thus, vulnerable writers need respectful response.

4. The author's chair supports the learning of all authors.

When authors share their work and receive feedback, the entire class, including the teacher, learns. A writer might share a story about going to the park with his or her family, causing a peer to be reminded of a similar story. Another writer might display the map he or she created within his or her informational text, and a peer might get ideas for including a similar map in a report about butterflies. Still another writer might write to persuade school administrators to broaden the menu of breakfast items available in the cafeteria, from which a teacher may learn that the child has a vested interest in the menu because it may be the only food the child eats that day. Indeed, the chair is for the specific response one writer needs, but an entire class benefits from the discussion.

5. The author's chair is not a place of transition but of transformation.

When students gather to share, this time is not meant to signal a transition from one curricular subject to the next. The author's chair experience can be just as informative as the mini-lesson and just as responsive as a conference. Often the chair becomes the place where powerful transformations happen. Yes, writers learn about writing. But more often, the audience learns about the writer. When this occurs, a richer, deeper, more connected community forms, and all learners are transformed because they become better known to others.

Writers Lead the Response Agenda

Think back to Thom and the story that began this chapter. What would we have learned if Thom had had choices as he sat in the author's chair? If Thom had directed the audience to affirm his writing, would that have told us he felt unsure about the second language he was still learning? What if Thom had sat in the chair and asked for *suggestions*? Maybe the class would have offered richer examples of the work Martin Luther King Jr. did to enact social change that involved more than just "sharing stuff." What if Thom had asked for *connections*, as in, "Guys, tell me what this reminds you of"? Perhaps his classmates would have shared stories of discrimination or of standing up for their values. Maybe, through the conversation, Thom would have connected the wave of social change made possible through the civil rights movement with the wave of social change that forced his family to leave Cambodia.

What if?

The author's chair is a richer, more authentic practice when writers drive the agenda. "This is what I need from you" becomes a powerful agentive stance that turns the chair into a powerful throne. The writer sits and shares, the audience listens and responds, and the entire class learns from the experience.

But the author's chair can be a befuddling experience for writers who are given this agency for the first time. Whether it's a kindergarten class or a graduate class, teachers begin the year by asking authors, "How do you want us to respond?" and authors typically say, "Oh, just say anything you want." But "anything" is too broad, and responders need direction. The default response is "I like [your story, your drawing]." When the audience is given "anything" as the choice, the response is seldom helpful. And sometimes, it's harmful. I've witnessed several author's chairs where young writers shared their published work with peers and, instead of praise, received revision suggestions. When an author shares a published piece of writing, the writer likely doesn't want to hear suggestions to improve it!

Authors who seek response come to the chair typically seeking the following types of responses: (1) responses that highlight their strengths as writers; (2) responses that help guide their processes as writers (suggestions for planning, revision, and editing); (3) responses that elicit ideas for writing; and (4) responses that show how they connect with other writers in the classroom. Let's look at each one of these within the contexts of real classrooms. (See Figure 2.1.)

Students Seek Response About Their Strengths.

Writers who ask "What did I do right in this piece of writing?" come to the chair seeking ways for the audience to note their strengths. When peers highlight strengths, they explain what's effective about the writing—confirming how an intended audience may be affected, verifying that the writer fulfilled his or her purpose, or highlighting the ways in which the author successfully navigated his or her process. Writers who seek response to highlight strengths may phrase their request in the following ways:

- "Please tell me a line you really remember." (Where was I successful in my use of description?)
- "Tell me what you thought about my characters." (Where was I successful in developing my characters?)

Author's Choices at the Author's Chair

How should the audience respond?

Compliments: What do you like about my writing?

Connections: How does my writing connect to your life?

Memorable lines: What's a line you really remember?

Questions: What questions do you have for me as a writer?

Suggestions: What changes do you think I should make?

Ideas: Help! I need help coming up with an idea!

Figure 2.1 Author's Choices at the Author's Chair

- "How do you think my [family, friends, community] will react to this piece of writing?" (How am I connecting with my intended audience?)
- "Tell me what you've learned from me." (Where did I successfully convey information about myself or something else?)
- "Tell me what makes this piece persuasive." (How was I effective in my use of persuasive techniques?)
- "Tell me how you feel after hearing this piece." (What was the emotional effect of the piece?)

To illustrate this, let's go into a classroom of second graders who just finished an informational unit on how-to writing. Students wrote drafts about different things they knew how to do. After several weeks, and multiple drafts, students chose one piece to take to publication. Their chosen piece went through a series of revisions and edits.

Students were particularly excited about the publication celebration connected with this unit. As a class, they decided to bring in materials and perform their how-to pieces in front of their peers at the author's chair. This gave authors an opportunity to teach their peers how to do something and provided an authentic purpose and audience for their writing.

Kate wrote "How to Make Hot Chocolate" and brought in the materials to perform it in front of her peers (Figure 2.2). Rather than sitting in the author's chair, she stood in front of it and performed each step of her how-to as her teacher read it aloud.

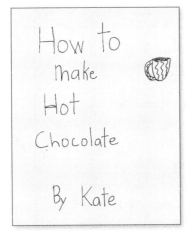
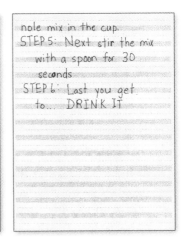

Figure 2.2 Kate's How-To book

Upon completion, she took a big swig of her hot chocolate, sighed a loud "Yum," and then asked the class to note her strengths. The author's chair response began with the teacher.

Teacher: Kate, what kind of response do you want from the class?

Kate: What do you think I did a good job on with my how-to?

Teacher: That's probably a good choice now that you're finished and it's published. Okay, we need some friends to tell Kate some good things she did as a writer.

[*Kate calls on Kevin.*]

Kevin: Well, you have all the steps in there. I mean . . . you didn't miss any of the steps, so you did a nice job making sure they were all in here.

[*Kate picks Malia next*]: I love that you picked hot chocolate. YUM!

Teacher, *expanding the response*: So you like her topic. You thought she did a nice job picking a topic that other people would be interested in reading about?

Malia: Yep. Now I'm ready to make some hot chocolate!

[*Brad jumps in*]: I kind of like how you put those steps on the page.

Kate: What do you mean?

Brad: Well, look how you wrote *STEP* on the page. I mean, it's the only word in your book that has all capital letters. So when you look at your book, you see where all the steps are on the page. It's really easy to see. Kinda cool. I should probably change mine to look like that!

In one short session, peers highlight Kate's strengths: (1) a fully developed informational text that's clear and comprehensive, (2) a topic that interests readers, and (3) the skill to incorporate text features that make the writing easy for the reader to read. When audience members highlight her strengths, Kate gains confidence. And as she shares in the author's chair, not only does she learn, but her fellow writing peers do as well.

Students Seek Response to Help Guide Their Process.

Many authors come to the author's chair in search of suggestions that take them closer to publication. When authors ask, "What can I do to make this writing better?" they are seeking constructive feedback that informs. They may look for ways to plan a piece so their writing has purpose and an authentic audience, or they may seek editing suggestions by placing their almost-finished writing under a document camera and peer-editing with the entire group. I've noticed that students are typically searching for revision suggestions and their author's chair agenda sounds something like this:

- "What parts are missing?"
- "Tell me which parts confused you."
- "Tell me where you got lost."
- "Tell me other ways I could begin this piece of writing."
- "During which part did your mind start to wander?"
- "Tell me how I should end my writing."
- "Tell me what information you still need to know."
- "Did I persuade you to think a certain way?"
- "What parts of my writing should I keep? What parts should I get rid of?"
- "What do you think is the *one* thing I'm trying to say with this piece of writing?"
- For young children, "What drawings should I add?"

When authors seek these types of responses, I ask them to come to the chair with open minds. I explain, "Your peers are going to give you some suggestions, but you are the decision maker. Some suggestions might help. Some might not be right for what you're trying to do as a writer. You'll need to listen carefully to see what might work."

For younger children, I write/draw peer responses on different sticky notes (Figure 2.3) and pass them to the author as he or she leaves the chair. I ask older writers to come to the chair with a pencil and daybook, and they take notes as the audience gives suggestions. Often, before the author leaves the chair, I summarize peer suggestions and might offer one of my own (Figure 2.4). I want authors to leave with fresh ideas that carry their writing forward into publication.

Figure 2.3 Sticky note of suggestions for a first grader's all-about book

Figure 2.4 Sticky note of suggestions for a fifth grader who is writing a story

Students Seek Response to Elicit Ideas for Writing.

I learned an important lesson from a reluctant writer during one writer's workshop. Andrew, a second grader, raised his hand, eager to share at the author's chair. I was teaching a writing unit on informational writing—specifically, teaching children how to write all-about books. When I looked at the paper in his hand, I said, "There's nothing on your page. How can you share when there's nothing on your page?"

Andrew stood, smiled, and walked confidently to the chair anyway. "You'll see, you'll see." He sat, held up his blank paper, and spoke. His classmates, familiar with the author's chair routine, knew how to respond.

Andrew: Look. Nothing. I need ideas, guys!

The class laughed. But once the laughter subsided, questions from peers emerged.

Sam: What's something you know a lot about?
Andrew: Sports.
Emily: Which sports?
Andrew: Oh, soccer, football, basketball.
Fred: Which of those do you like the best?
Andrew: Hmm . . .
Sarah: Well, which one do you know the most about?
Andrew: Probably soccer.
Sarah: Well, then, that's what you should write about.

This conversation continued for five minutes. Once peers helped Andrew narrow down a topic, they brainstormed various subtopics he could write about in his all-about book. They suggested a page on soccer rules, another about different professional soccer teams, and another about famous soccer players. One student suggested that he could bring in how-to writing and explain to readers how to kick a ball. By the time Andrew left the chair, he had a collection of ideas to use and used the momentum of the response to get him moving as a writer.

There's something magical in an interaction in which a student teaches me something I never considered a possibility. Andrew taught me this: *The author's chair is not just a place for celebration; it's also a place for germination.* Ideas don't always come easily to writers—some topics come from seed ideas passed across the carpet from other writers whose suggestions provide possibilities for authors to consider.

In the midst of our own learning from the writers, we can document what we notice from the interaction. We ask ourselves, "What did I learn from Andrew's author's chair exchange? What did I learn about Andrew? What did I learn about my students' knowledge about generating ideas? And how can I use this to guide future mini-lessons and conferences?" Then we use our notes to guide future instruction. Many times, the response that happens in the author's chair, and our subsequent reflection on that response, makes us reexamine our lesson plans and adjust them accordingly (see the appendix for tips to help students generate ideas for writing).

Students Seek Response to Make Connections.

When I think about why students choose compliments for their responses, I'm reminded of a fifth-grade student named Consuela who had little confidence as a writer among a classroom of students who wrote enthusiastically. She showed this lack of confidence in the frown she wore every time writer's workshop began. She struggled to put anything down on the page, and when she did, it didn't look like the writing of her peers. It looked more like the type of writing many first graders compose. Consuela knew this, and it embarrassed her.

Consuela seldom wanted to sit in the author's chair, until one day she did. Her class was in the middle of a writing unit about biography—and she decided to write an autobiography. The words bled onto the page: a section about her neighborhood, another about her friends, a half page about her twin sister, and two lines about her absent dad. Finally, an entire page about her mom. Her life was scribed across two and a half pages of effort.

"I want compliments on this one," she directed the class.

When the compliments came in abundance, a huge smile swept across her face. Consuela finally felt like a fellow member of this active writing community.

In another third-grade classroom, Erik and I had a powerful conference. He read a story he wrote about playing football at his family reunion. His writing focused on his father, brothers, uncles, and cousins, and the football game they played. He talked about his sisters being the cheerleaders and his mom under the shelter preparing lunch and his grandmother and aunties helping. After Erik read it to me, I asked, "What do you think this story is *really* about?"

Erik looked at me, perplexed. I continued, "I mean, I know you're writing about football and you're playing this game with your family, and everyone is around doing their thing. But why did you choose to write about this day? It seems like it's just any old day to me."

Click. Erik got it. He looked downward and muttered, "It's the only day my whole family is together—me, my mom, my dad, my sisters, and brothers."

I asked, "So, you don't all live together?"

Erik replied, "Nope. Me and my brothers live with my dad. My sisters live with my mom."

I got it.

I asked Erik if he would be willing to share in the author's chair, and he agreed. He asked the class to connect to his piece of writing. A couple of students talked about their family reunions, and a couple more talked about football. But then, Armando spoke.

Armando: Just like my life.

Brian: What do you mean?

Armando: Well, my family is all split up, too. Haven't seen my mama since she left. So, I feel you.

Armando got it, too.

Sometimes, children come to the author's chair seeking not just the worthiness of their writing but also a worthiness of self. In classrooms where we engage in the

Digital Diversion: Broadening the Author's Audience

The author's chair is essentially a classroom space authors use to seek response. But the chair is not limited to classroom walls. Teachers across the country are finding digital ways to help authors broaden their audiences. The following table describes various digital possibilities for author's chair.

DIGITAL TOOL	HOW IT CAN BE USED FOR AUTHOR'S CHAIR	RECOMMENDED SITES
Wikis	Teachers create a wiki page for each student in the class to serve as a writing portfolio. Students upload artifacts onto their wiki pages. Then they ask audiences (classmates and parents) to respond in specific ways.	PBWorks WikiSpaces LiveBinders
Blogs	As with a classroom bulletin board, students choose a piece of writing that they think shows something important they learned as a writer and ask the teacher to post it on the class blog (or, for older students, their own blog). Other students and parents can post supportive comments about that piece as feedback for the writer.	Edublogs Tumblr Shutterfly
Social Networking Sites	Many teachers are harnessing the power of social networking to communicate with parents by maintaining a class Twitter feed, Instagram feed, Facebook page, and Pinterest board. Again, a writer can post a piece of writing to one of these sites and ask others to give specific response to their work.	Twitter Facebook Instagram Pinterest

Through digital technology, response is more public and instant—with advantages and disadvantages to both. Suddenly, writers recognize how wide the potential audience might be for their work. Instead of twenty to twenty-five readers, there is now the potential for hundreds and thousands of readers. And instead of response controlled by the writer, the digital reader may give feedback that is not necessarily wanted—making writers more vulnerable than ever. Interestingly, the designers of wikis and blog sites recognize the importance of authors' controlling response. That's why they give authors the power to delete comments made by others before they go public. Yes, even designers within the Internet—the unregulated Wild West of information dissemination—recognize the importance of giving the authority back to the writer.

vulnerable work of speaking about our lives, sometimes the writing is secondary to the yearning students seek to be accepted, to be heard, and to be loved. To be connected. Yes, the author's chair is a place for the writer to get response. But it can also be a powerful space where writers can get comfort from a community who cares.

Writers Guide the Teacher's Choices

I've discovered that supportive response, directed by the author, is awkward at first. When response becomes a possibility, authors aren't sure how to direct their readers, and readers aren't sure how to respond appropriately. When this happens, teachers quickly become decision makers. They ask themselves these kinds of questions:

- *What procedures have I set in place so authors receive the feedback they need and audiences offer it in constructive ways?*
- *Where is my voice in this process, and when do I need to insert myself into the author's chair conversation?*
- *How do I document what authors need, how audiences respond to the author, and what authors do with that response?*
- *In what ways do authors teach me when they sit in the chair?*
- *How broadly can we go as writers to reach wide audiences with our writing?*

In many ways, the writer's workshop is a continuum that goes from mostly teacher driven (the mini-lesson) to teacher *and* student driven (conferring) to mostly student driven (author's chair and reflection). But even though writers direct the author's chair, teachers have an important role in establishing, guiding, and supporting the process. More important, teachers must model this through their own response to writers.

Students Show Us Procedures to Teach.

Whether we're teaching kindergartners or graduate students, we should reserve the beginning part of the year for procedures—a series of lessons that say, "This is how things are done in our classroom." These lessons are derived from studying students and, honestly, asking, "What are my students doing in my classroom that's driving me nuts?" Those are usually the lessons that we need to teach right away so we don't run off course from the lessons that help students become better writers. Among the lessons about pencil sharpening, daybook organizing, and conference behaviors, we should weave in at least three or four mini-lessons focused entirely on the author's chair. These mini-lessons show writers and responders (1) ways authors speak when in the chair, (2) ways in which an audience listens respectfully, (3) types of response authors may ask for from the audience, and (4) how audiences respond to the author based on the author's agenda.

The list above is not exhaustive. Depending on the age of the students and the innovative things we're doing in the classroom, we sprinkle in other lessons throughout the year to support the response agenda. But these lessons don't usually come until after we've spent some time together in the classroom and had the opportunity to think reflectively about how response in the chair is progressing. To put it a different way, students teach us what else they need us to teach.

Consider asking students to keep a written record (in daybooks) of what they have learned from their fellow writers. Or consider a digital tool (like wikis or blogs) to use as a running record of suggestions. When using new tools, we need to teach another series of lessons about how to use the technology and appropriate ways to respond to authors within digital spaces. We have to be responsive with our lessons, because we teach according to the changing needs of our students.

Students should have easy access to these procedures; many teachers type mini-lessons in kid-friendly language, print them on half sheets of paper, and ask students to glue them in their daybooks. The examples provided in the appendix can be used or modified based on the age of the children you teach. For younger students, I've seen teachers use actual photographs to illustrate each point or make movies of students one year to show to new students the following year. Then, to offer continued support, teachers create anchor charts to hang in the room and provide refresher lessons whenever necessary.

Students Make Room for Teachers to Add Their Voices to the Author's Chair.

Although the author's chair is author driven, and the responses come almost entirely from peers, sometimes teachers must insert their voices to clarify, define, redirect, and summarize. This was the case when first grader Michelle sat in the chair.

Michelle began, "Okay, I want you to tell me what you like about my story." She read her memoir about game night and awaited peer response.

"I like that you wrote about game night," Sofia said.

I pushed her a little: "Why do you like that she wrote about game night?"

"I like playing games, too," Sofia said. "So that's why I liked it."

"Sounds like you're making a connection to Michelle's topic, Sofia," I said, to clarify.

Sofia nodded. I turned to Michelle and offered, "Michelle, I think you hit on something important as a writer. You wrote about something that other writers in this class connect to. That's a pretty powerful thing to do as a writer."

Ander raised his hand, and Michelle called on him.

"I like how you put in those bubbles when people are talking," he said.

"Thanks," Michelle replied.

"Yeah," Ander continued. "I do the same thing in my books."

I delved more deeply. "I notice that many of you make those bubbles in the stories you write in this class. Those are called speech bubbles. It's a writer's trick to show the audience who's talking. Mo Willems does that in *Don't Let the Pigeon Drive the Bus!* Since so many of you are drawing these great stories, speech bubbles are a nice way to show what your characters are thinking and saying."

We continued with this type of dialogue for about two or three minutes. A student offered an initial response, the writer gave thanks for the response, and, when necessary, I took the opportunity to deepen the response by clarifying, defining, or naming the craft the writer was exhibiting in his or her work. Students who have never offered responses in the past often give rudimentary responses at first. This is true with our youngest writers who are still developing as language users. But it's also true for our older writers who have never been in writing classrooms where they were asked to assert their voice. Writers need models of reflective voices, and teachers can provide those models when the need arises. And when you see an opportunity to model a deeper response, go for it.

Teachers Document the Author's Chair and Reflect on What Students Teach Us.

If the author's chair is a powerful space where authors and audiences learn, it's also a powerful space for teachers to learn about students. Teachers who make the bold decision to document interactions at the author's chair collect rich, informative data. Consider the insights that are gained when teachers document this process. Teachers learn the following:

- The type of response the author elicited from peers
- The varied ways audience members gave those responses
- Who offered feedback (and who didn't)
- The quality of feedback offered
- Instructional implications of the response

There are many different ways to document conversations that take place at the author's chair, but two you should consider are the Author's Chair Documentation Log and the Audience Response Map. Both documents serve three purposes: (1) they capture the exchanges that take place among students and show whether the feedback given was, indeed, the feedback desired by the author; (2) they provide insight into what students have learned so far as writers and what they have yet to learn; and (3) they offer a road map informing teachers where to go next for mini-lessons and conferences.

I use the Author's Chair Documentation Log (see Figure 2.5; reproducible in appendix) to show who has shared at the author's chair, the type of response they ask

Author's Chair

Teacher Documentation

AUTHOR/ DATE	TYPE OF RESPONSE SOUGHT	WHAT I NOTICE	INSTRUCTIONAL IMPLICATIONS
Liam 10/27/14	Compliments	Liam asked class to give him revision suggestions for his memoir about the beach. The beach is his most important place. Students suggested he add more details about the place. "Why was it so important?" the students wondered. "Make me feel like I was there," Laaisa says. "Add sensory details," Amaya says. These were great suggestions! The kids are remembering our revision strategies.	Felica mentioned ways to develop the setting. Hmm . . . haven't done a lesson on this yet. We've done one on developing characters. Okay, think I'll do a setting one. Which authors should I choose? —Jane Yolen is a good one. Love how she did the setting in *Owl Moon.* —Karen Hesse paints a nice picture of NYC in *Come On, Rain!*
Marcus 10/27/14	Suggestions	Marcus asked the class to give him revision suggestions for his informational text about basketball. Several students told him he should include a list of stats about different players. We talked about including informational text features like graphics and call-out boxes that might contain extra information.	Oh, I need to pull some different magazines and books that include different and unusual informational text features. We need to study those!
Talia 10/28/14	Connections	Talia shared a memoir about going on a trip with just her mom. Wanted the class to connect. Why connection? The piece is just a draft and there's much more for her to add. Not quite sure why she would select a connection response.	Hmm . . . maybe a mini-lesson about making purposeful choices in the author's chair. Need to demonstrate how authors might choose a type of response purposefully rather than randomly.

Figure 2.5 Author's Chair Documentation Log

for, snippets of the response they get from peers, and reflections about how I might use the response in future mini-lessons or conference sessions. When I take notes, I think about the following:

- **Who is sharing:** *This ensures that all writers in my classroom have an opportunity to sit in the chair at least once or twice a month.*

- **The type of response the author seeks:** *This allows me to analyze the writer to find patterns. I may ask, "Is this student seeking the same type of response every time? If so, why?" And it may lead me to make suggestions for the author to try a different type of response next time he or she sits in the chair.*
- **What I notice from the interaction:** *By writing notes, I can begin to see the type of response other students give to the writer. I may ask, "Are they responding in the way the author asked? Are they paying attention? Are they giving responses that fulfill the writer's need?" Again, I can use this documentation to have conversations with responders—acknowledging thoughtful, helpful response, and giving suggestions to those struggling to respond to the writer.*
- **The instructional implications for the class:** *When I record these notes, the author's chair becomes another formative assessment space for me. I see possibilities for future mini-lessons and directions I might go in for future conferences with students.*

I use the Audience Response Map (see Figure 2.6) three to four times a month specifically to analyze the interactions that occur among the responders. I chart the names

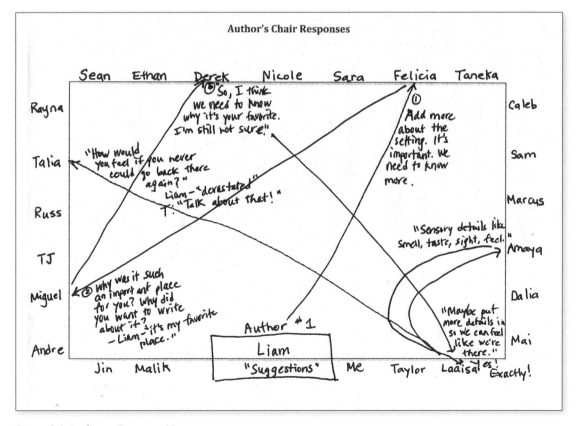

Figure 2.6 Audience Response Maps

of the students and where they sit on the floor. Then, as they begin giving responses, I make notations about who speaks (and who doesn't), who keeps the conversation going, the type of feedback given, and who gets called on to share. Upon analysis of this map, I reflect on the following:

- Are all students getting picked to offer responses, or is it just a few students who respond each time?
- Which students *never* offer a response to the author? Why?
- Who listens to the responses of others and adds to them?
- Who takes the responses in an entirely different direction?
- What kind of response do they offer? Is it useful for the author?

Collecting these authentic forms of formative assessment provides counternarratives to the mandated state assessments that often define our students in narrow and fractured ways. Our notes tell stories that reveal the nuanced, complicated, and messy ways our students think and learn. Teachers take notes, study them, and know their students better because of their record keeping. In fact, collecting this documentation, analyzing, and reflecting upon its meaning is probably the most important choice a teacher makes in the classroom.

Frequently Asked Questions About Author's Chair

1. What do I do when everyone wants to share at the author's chair?

As much as I love the energy and enthusiasm of an entire classroom that wants to share (sadly, this enthusiasm sometimes wanes as kids grow older), we have time for only two or three students to share during each class meeting. But I don't want to dismiss this enthusiasm, so I often have students turn and talk to a partner so at least someone hears about their writing that day!

2. What are some effective ways to manage who shares at the author's chair?

I've seen teachers use all sort of effective strategies to quickly see who has and hasn't shared. Here are some of my favorites:

Tape a class list to the back of the chair and cross off the names of those who have already had an opportunity to share.

Place a class-at-a-glance grid on a clipboard near the chair and mark an *X* next to the name of the author who shared.

Use wooden craft sticks and two empty cans, one marked "Yet to Share," the other marked "Already Shared." Draw a name from one can and place it in the other after that student has shared.

3. *How do I handle the frustration of those students who don't get picked for the author's chair?*

I harness the energy students have for sharing by asking them to turn and talk to a writing buddy before author's chair begins. That way, they get response from at least one other person. Typically, this satisfies those who were disappointed they didn't get picked in the first place.

4. *Most students want to share, but I have some students who never want to share. Do I force them to share anyway?*

This is always a tough call for me. I want all the students to experience what it's like to share, but I don't want author's chair to be something I force students to do. I usually do some conferring in this situation. I try to find out why students are hesitant to share:

- Are they afraid of peer response?
- Do they lack confidence as a writer?
- Do they think their writing isn't as good as their peers'?
- Are they shy? Fearful? Worried?
- Are their topics too personal? Or do they think their topic selection is substandard?

Then I'll ask casually, "Okay, what's the real reason you don't want to share?" Once I find out the real reason, I troubleshoot. I typically manage to find a pathway to the chair that makes writers feel comfortable. I might see something a student is doing well, highlight it, and suggest he or she share. Or I might say, "You don't seem too sure about this. Why don't you just put it out there to others in the class to see what they think?"

For shy students, the author's chair may be a frightful place. I resist forcing children to share at the chair. Instead I offer alternatives that might alleviate some of their trepidation. For example, I might say, "If you sit in the chair, I'll do most of the talking." At the very least, I want them to know the feeling of the chair and to have the experience of seeing the faces of an audience. For these children, I try to make the experience of being in the chair as supportive, nurturing, and positive as I can, with the hope that they will exit the chair wanting to revisit sometime soon.

5. *When writers ask for suggestions, I think some suggestions are wrong and others would make the writing worse if the author used them. What do I do in those situations?*

I step in and politely challenge the responder to think deeply about their suggestion. I might say, "Do you think that suggestion will make this a better piece of writing, or do you think it will make it more confusing for the reader?" I ask the writer what she thinks about the suggestion. And I ask other audience members to give their opinions. Usually, this turns into a rich discussion about what writers do to make their writing clearer, more concise, and more accessible to readers. And I try to do it in a respectful way. Just as it is risky for the author to sit in the chair, it's risky for the responder. So, although I acknowledge all responses, I always try to challenge them if the suggestions are way off base.

6. *Shouldn't I use the author's chair to reinforce my mini-lesson?*

In her powerful essay titled "The Author's Chair Revisited," Cynthia McCallister (2008) says, "I suggest that by using the author's chair to exclusively recognize children who execute and apply skills that have just been taught and reinforced, teachers inadvertently honor conformity rather than the process of making the kind of carefully considered, personally relevant, sagacious decisions that characterized the process of capable writers" (461). To this I say, Amen! This is the author's space, not the teacher's. The author sets the agenda. I had my opportunity to teach during the mini-lesson. The author's chair gives authors the "author"ity to drive the audience, to take us in unexpected directions, to teach us lessons we haven't yet considered. And therein lies the power of the chair.

Travelogue

Like many teachers, I did not always see the value of the author's chair in my own classroom, so if time was limited, the author's chair got the old heave-ho. But I now see the author's chair as something bigger than just an author sharing writing. Author's chair deepens other characteristics within our students that can expand across the curriculum and beyond the classroom walls. It gives permission for learners to take risks, be courageous, accept constructive feedback, offer support, think critically, reflect, and make connections—all qualities we want students to carry from their classroom lives to their out-of-the-classroom lives.

Recently, I published an article in *Reading Matters* (Kissel, Stover, and Glover 2014) in which I tell the story of Nikki, a student in my graduate class who was also a teacher at a local school. My graduate students write multigenre life stories as a way to explore their writing selves. They choose a topic, establish their own purpose for writing about it, and determine audiences for a collection of writings that examine their topic using multiple genres. Ultimately, they learn how to teach writing by reflecting on their own writing habits, processes, and experiences.

Nikki took my class at a time when she was feeling emotionally vulnerable. Just weeks before the semester began, her best friend had been murdered, shot dead in his neighborhood by an unstable neighbor. Nikki chose to base her multigenre life story on the life and death of her friend. She wrote several pieces in varied genres, but one piece was particularly powerful. She composed a letter to the man who killed her friend, telling him all about the life he had so dismissively taken away from the world.

I asked Nikki, "Do you think you'll ever send this letter to him?" At the time she said she had written it just for herself.

Not long after Nikki composed the letter, the man was brought to trial. Character witnesses were asked to take the stand to talk about the life of the man he had killed. It was an opportunity to show jurors who Nikki's friend was—more than a victim of a horrible crime. Nikki saw this as her opportunity—a real-life chance to read her letter in a different type of author's chair.

Nikki sat in the witness chair, faced the killer, and directed the response. "I want you to know about my friend, about the life you took away from me and others who loved him so much. I want you to listen and know what you've done."

Nikki read. Tears streamed down her face. The killer never met her gaze, but he *heard* her words. So did the jurors. A few days later, the jurors sentenced the man to prison for decades.

I suppose an author's chair isn't always limited to a seat in the middle of a classroom. It may just be a small, uncomfortable chair in the middle of a courtroom—a place where an author has something profound to say and an attentive audience who needs to hear it. Nikki lost a friend who would never be replaced. But she also found something: her voice. That was a powerful lesson for Nikki to learn.

Chapter 3

Reflection: Writers Ponder the Journey

I n the midst of working within a classroom of fourth graders, I interview children three months into the school year about their writing habits. They have been engaged in a daily writer's workshop, and many of their drafts, plans, ideas, notes, and musings are crafted in a marble composition book Donald Murray (2004) calls a daybook and Aimee Buckner (2013) calls a writer's notebook. I approach one boy, Lucas, and ask him to reflect on the contents of his daybook. Lucas talks about the ideas he wrote across several pages. He points out several "glue-ins" his teacher gave him—her mini-lessons typed and printed on half sheets of paper so students can use them as references. He shows his drawings, his plans, and the page of memorable lines he gathered from reading—lines he thinks about imitating in his own writing.

After flipping through the pages for several minutes and describing his daybook, Lucas pauses. He grows quiet. He contemplates. Silence. Then, he speaks: "I guess, if I really think about it, well, not only is my writer's notebook a place for me to write down things about my life; it's like a textbook I create for myself." This is the insightfulness Lucas gained when granted a few minutes to ponder.

If we think of our children as complex, nuanced, multidimensional learners, then the way we assess them must be varied as well. Think of assessment as a mosaic composed of several colors and shapes of glass that form the full picture of our students' learning. Personal reflection on writing adds vibrant colors and interesting shapes that allow that mosaic to shimmer. This radiance doesn't usually occur in standardized forms of assessment.

When we are in the thick of learning, we are so busy building the mosaic, we seldom have a chance to step back to see the shape it's taking. Reflection allows us to take in the aerial view. As Lucas suggests, reflection pushes us to "really think about" what we know. Review my guiding beliefs about reflection and take a few minutes to ponder your own beliefs about the role reflection plays in your writing instruction—and in your personal writing.

Guiding Beliefs About Reflection

The following beliefs reveal my understanding of reflection. These beliefs guide my practice in classrooms and keep me focused on the purpose for reflection:

1. *Reflection reveals voice.*

When we allow students to speak or write their thoughts about themselves as writers—their influences, their progress, their feelings—we empower them to add their voices to an assessment profile that reveals the complexity of what they know. Often, we make judgments about our learners using various assessments designed by others. But when writers reflect, we get rich insight into their thinking. They voice what they know. And we learn more about them as writers as a result.

2. *Writers use an internal compass when they reflect.*

When writers reflect, they use an internal compass to guide their revelations. They look back, look forward, look inward, and look outward. As they scan the terrain of their writing experiences, reflection gives them direction about where they've been and where they need to go next.

3. *Reflection needs a place in the daily writing routine.*

When writers reflect daily, they leave a workshop naming how they spent their writing time, how the experience felt, who influenced their learning, and what they plan to do in the future. Reflection allows writers to focus—to say, "This is how I've changed as a writer today." Teachers should leave a couple of minutes at the end of a workshop to allow writers to engage in and record their reflective thinking.

4. *Reflection counters the testing narrative.*

Too often, only one story is told about our students—a narrative told by a test, given on a single day, designed and graded by someone (or some machine) who does not know the child. We get incomplete snapshots of children's learning. Reflection, when guided by writers, counters the testing narratives. When our writers reflect daily, monthly, and throughout the academic year, they get opportunities to tell us fuller, richer stories of their literate lives.

Reflection as Part of the Assessment Landscape

Recently, I met with a group of teachers grappling with literacy assessment. They wanted to figure out what the assessment data said about their students and what it meant for instruction. To begin our inquiry, I asked teachers to brainstorm a list of all the assessments students experienced in a given year:

- Beginning-of-grade assessment (state standardized assessment)
- End-of-grade assessment (state standardized assessment)
- Dynamic Indicators of Basic Early Literacy Skills
- Developmental Reading Assessment
- Phonological Awareness Literacy Screening
- Standardized Reading Inventory
- Diagnostic Reading Assessment
- Running records
- Teacher-created reading tests
- Writing prompts graded via rubric
- Conference notes

We conservatively estimated that teachers spent roughly forty instructional days' worth of time assessing. Teachers of younger children argued it was closer to sixty days. Almost two months spent assessing!

Next, I passed out a blank array of boxes and asked teachers to write each assessment in a separate box. Using scissors, teachers made a stack of cards. We sorted the cards in a variety of ways. First, we sorted by types of assessment: diagnostic, formative, and summative. Then we sorted the assessments into formal and informal types. Finally, I asked teachers to sort the assessments into three categories: state created, teacher created, and student created. Teachers easily pushed cards into the first two categories. But there was nothing under the "student-created" category.

A teacher noticed: "Our kids have no voice in any of this." Bingo!

Our students spend hours completing assessments created for them but don't spend one second speaking for themselves. Shouldn't they have a say in all this? And shouldn't their voices be the loudest?

Reflection as the Counternarrative to Standardized Testing

Assessment is important. It provides snapshots of what students may or may not know on a given day. Some standardized assessments provide teachers initial direction into areas that may require instructional emphasis. They can provide insight. But when too much focus is put on standardized assessments, only some of the learner's story gets told. In the hustle and bustle of moving through standards, pushing through curricula, meeting deadlines, and preparing for high-stakes tests, students seldom engage in self-assessment. Reflection has become the missing piece of the writer's workshop—and maybe in students' entire daily routine.

In her research focused on growth mindsets, Carol Dweck (2007) found that students' perceptions of themselves as learners play a big role in their success at school. Giving students time and space to thoughtfully examine their work, provide feedback, and evaluate their learning makes learners realize the developmental nature of their intellectual abilities. In other words, intelligence is not fixed (Yeager and Dweck 2012). And, when writers are equipped with blank pieces of paper, sharpened pencils, and opportunities to assess their own learning, they give us access to their thinking (Yancy 1998). When this happens, writers reclaim something standardized testing has taken away: their voices.

Reflection needs to play a prominent role in the writer's workshop. After the mini-lesson, conference, and author's chair, students and teachers can consider what was learned that day. Students can be empowered to leave the group area and consider, *What is something I learned today as a writer?* Think how much we can learn about our students by analyzing those responses.

Reflecting Daily, Monthly, and Yearly

The school year presents multiple opportunities for reflection: daily reflections, monthly reflections, quarterly reflections, and yearly reflections. And these reflections can take multiple forms:

- Daily reflections: one- to two-minute quick-writes or quick-shares
- Monthly reflections: setting, monitoring, and meeting goals
- Quarterly and yearly reflections: portfolios

When writers reflect daily, each day presents an opportunity for them to name their learning. When writers reflect throughout the month, they realize the importance of setting goals and of working toward achieving those goals over a series of weeks. When writers reflect over the course of a quarter and an entire year, they learn about the cumulative nature of learning and the transformation that occurs over long swaths of time. Collectively, when given short bursts of time each day, each month, and each quarter to engage in reflection, writers emerge as more knowledgeable about themselves than they were before entering the classroom. Teachers gain insight about their students' growth as writers, their challenges when writing, and their goals going forward. And this reflection provides rich assessment data about students as writers.

Daily Reflections: Reflective Quick-Writes and Quick-Shares

The end of the workshop is an ideal time to ask students to think about themselves as writers. They have just engaged in writing for a chunk of time, and their experiences are fresh in their minds. After author's chair, consider asking writers to do a quick-write or a quick-share that is focused on their learning. They may open their daybooks and write about it on a blank page or section devoted to reflection. Or they may turn and talk to a peer, keeping in mind a focused question.

Of course, reflection should be open ended and driven by the writer. But the teacher may consider giving some guidance on the type of reflection. Teachers can ask writers to look back, look forward, look inward, and look outward.

Looking Back

Looking back engages writers in the assessment process of examining their habits, processes, and resourcefulness during the workshop time. You can first model this process by reflecting on your own writing moves when you share your work with the class. After students have seen how you assess your own work, they have an idea of how they might do it when they think about their own learning.

At the end of a workshop experience, one kindergarten class engaged in the following conversation:

> Teacher: During our mini-lesson today I wrote about my mom and our trip to the department store when I was younger. Remember, I got lost! Oh boy, was I scared. When I look back on what I did as a writer today, I realize that I really added how I felt to the story. I don't know if I've done that in previous things I've written. I can now add feelings to my writing. I want you to think back about what you did as a writer. Turn to a friend and share something you did when you wrote today.
>
> [*Students turn and talk.*]
>
> Teacher: Let's gather back together and share with the whole group. Can someone share what you did today when you wrote?
>
> Sam: I made a book about soldiers.
>
> Teacher: Why did you choose to write about soldiers?
>
> Sam: I think they are cool.
>
> Teacher: That's great. You found something you're interested in writing about and went for it! Yes!
>
> Eve: I wrote all my letters.

Teacher: Why did you do that today as a writer?

Eve: I'm practicing. I'm trying to get better at them.

Teacher: Awesome! I think it's so smart to use some of your writing time to work on getting better at something. Good job.

The conversation goes on for another few minutes as the teacher continuously elicits reflective responses from the children. They announce something they did as a writer, the teacher affirms it, and the writers begin to realize the importance of thinking about their process.

Again, if reflection is self-examination, then we need to begin emphasizing reflection with our youngest writers. It's a form of self-assessment that will serve them well as they continue to develop as writers. Reflection is a developmental skill that deepens as students grow in age.

When asking students to look back, consider the following questions for quick-writes or quick-shares:

- "What did you end up doing as a writer today?" (See Figure 3.1a.)
- "Looking back, how did you spend your time today as a writer?"
- "What struggles did you have today as a writer?" (See Figure 3.1b.)
- "What successes did you have today as a writer?"
- "Looking back across your year so far, what have you noticed about yourself as a writer?"
- "Who helped you today? How did that person help?"

Figure 3.1a (left) A kindergartner draws a reflective picture of what he did during workshop time and says, "Me and my friends played blocks. We made a tower. [*Points to the M and the arrow.*] And we wrote elevator buttons. Going up!"

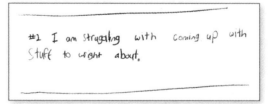

Figure 3.1b (above) A second grader reflects on the struggles he experienced during writer's workshop.

When writers reflect, they think about the immediate experience or learning that occurred over the course of the workshop. It delivers this message to writers: every day is an opportunity to learn something new during workshop time, and when given time to reflect, writers have the authority to name their learning. Teachers then have the opportunity to glean insight from these reflections when they read them. If, for example, a child struggles to come up with writing topics as the child in Figure 3.1b notes, the teacher can craft a specific conference with the child to help brainstorm ideas. This is how teachers can begin to see students' reflections as valuable bits of assessment data to drive instruction.

Looking Forward

Writers who look forward make plans for what they will do in future workshops. These types of questions prepare writers for the work that lies before them, helps them set daily goals for themselves, and encourages them to think about ways they can improve their craft. Consider asking the following questions as quick-writes or quick-shares to help students assess their plans:

- "In what ways do you hope to improve as a writer?"
- "What's one thing you want to improve in the piece of writing you worked on today?"
- "When you start writing again tomorrow, what's one thing you are going to change about your piece?"
- "In what ways do you want to grow as a writer?"
- "What are your plans for the rest of this genre study?" (See Figure 3.2.)
- "What are your strengths as a writer that you plan to carry forward into future pieces of writing?"
- "What's one thing you have seen from your peers that you would like to try in future pieces of writing?"
- "What's a goal you would like to set for yourself next time?"

When we ask writers to look forward, we deliver this message: a writer's work is continuous and recursive—and never done. Even when a piece has been published, writers can always ask themselves, *What should I do differently next time?*

Looking forward

the Book im working on for this week is the Halloween tale: Gohsts Book 2.

CHAPTERS
- the mystery in the mannor House.
- vanishing acts
- Lucys grave
- the portal to the underworld
- trixy has a party

Figure 3.2 A third grader looks forward by making plans for an upcoming book.

Looking Inward

Writing requires honest self-examination. Because we write about our lives—or about our perspective on the world around us—writing is an especially personal endeavor. When we look inward, we examine how our writing evokes feelings within us and how our processes as writers are affecting our psyche. Consider asking these questions for quick-writes and quick-shares:

- "How do you feel about the work you did today as a writer? What did you like? Dislike? Why?"
- "How did writing make you feel today? Think about drawing a picture of your face and using one word to describe it."
- "How did you feel about your process today?"
- "What did you learn about yourself as a writer today?"
- "What did you learn about yourself as a person from writing today?"
- "What does your writing topic reveal about you as a writer?"
- "How are you changing as a writer this year?"

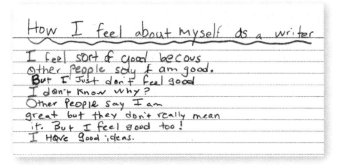

Figure 3.3 A third grader reflects on her feelings about being a writer.

When we ask writers to look inward, we send this message: being a writer will generate conflicting feelings of vulnerability, introspection, and worry, and reflection can be one way to mindfully acknowledge those feelings.

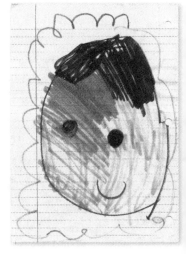

Figure 3.4 A kindergartner draws how he feels about his writing today (happy) and says, "I think I made a really good book today."

When students reflect on their feelings, teachers gain insight into their thinking that is not always present on a draft or revision of students' writing. Teachers can make note of writers' feelings about themselves and confer with them about it. For example, if children feel inadequate as writers (see Figure 3.3), teachers can show the ways in which they are prospering. When children note their happiness with what they did as writers (see Figure 3.4), teachers learn they are creating an environment that is conducive to writing. When students make concrete their inner feelings about worth and adequacy (see Figure 3.5), a window cracks open for the teacher to engage in richer, deeper, more meaningful discussions during conferring.

Reflection #6: How I've Changed

- Describe how you have changed this year as a writer. Here are some things to think about:
  - o In what ways are you a better writer this year than last year?
  - o What have you learned that you will remember to keep doing next year?
  - o Have your feelings changed about writing from last year to this year? If so, how?

I think I've grown as a writer in lots of ways. Last year, I didn't know a lot of genres to write about. But now that I've learned a lot about other genres, I have a wider selection of things to write. I'm also not as afraid to write my real feelings from my heart. I'll remember that a good thing to do is write without picking up your pencil and write without even thinking. I feel like I'm an even better writer this year than last because I'm smarter. And I always love how many compliments my teachers give me. And I have memories of my second grade teacher crying when she read my piece.

Figure 3.5 A fifth grader looks back on her year as a writer.

Looking Outward

Our written work is constantly judged. Anyone who places his or her eyes on the writing we produce forms opinions about the work. It's happening now as you read this book. Throughout the writing of this book, I have been constantly worried about the audience reading it. I worry how you will interpret my writing, if my words will make a difference in your teaching, how my peers will view my work, if my editor will like it, and how the publisher's team will view this book compared with others on a similar topic. Writers might address the following questions via quick-writes or quick-shares to look outward from their work:

- "Who has influenced you as a writer?" (See Figure 3.6.)
- "How do you think your writing is different from the way other people write?"
- "If you were the teacher, what would you write on a sticky note and leave on your piece of writing?"
- "What is a word (or phrase or line or section or paragraph) you think others will really notice when they read this piece of writing?"
- "According to your self-assessment, in what ways are you meeting the standards listed?"

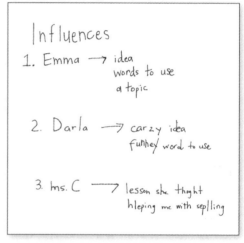

Figure 3.6 A third grader reflects on her writing influences.

- "When you look at your self-assessment, in what ways do you think you should improve your writing?"
- "In what ways have mentor authors supported you as a writer?" (See Figure 3.7.)

Figure 3.7 A third grader reflects on mentor authors who have supported her writing.

Writing is scary—because when it's published, it's public. Our students feel similarly. Asking them to look outward sends this message to writers: your work will be judged by others. How does it stack up?

Managing Daily Reflections

Teachers should reserve the last couple of minutes of the workshop to engage students in reflection so it becomes a routine, necessary component. Children in K–1 classrooms typically do this reflective work verbally; the teacher circles around the group area and listens in as peers turn and talk to one another. Children in grades 2–5 typically write these reflections in their daybooks and make a record of their thinking on paper. They may reserve a section in their daybook where reflections accumulate. Over time, students (and their teachers) can see how their thinking evolves.

To keep the reflection questions available to writers, you can create anchor charts with children and hang them around the room (see Figure 3.8). Writers add more questions to the charts over the course of the year as the questions naturally

Figure 3.8 Anchor chart of "looking back" questions

arise. Teachers may also make daybook sheets with reflection questions for children to paste in their daybooks (see the appendix for a sample). This makes reflection readily available to students and lets *them* choose which question(s) to ponder.

Finally, language matters. And what we say to spur reflection within our children can make a difference in their learning lives. Peter Johnston, in his awe-inspiring book *Choice Words* (2004), said it best when he described why he chose to write a book that recognizes the importance of how teachers talk in the classroom:

> My initial interest was in how teachers' use of language might explain their students' success in becoming literate, as documented on literacy tests. However, I frequently watched teachers accomplish remarkable things with their students and at the end of the day express guilt about their failure to accomplish some part of the curriculum. This guilt was, in my view, both unfounded and unproductive. It was caused, in part, by the teachers' inability to name all the things they *did* accomplish. (2)

Teachers can use words and phrases to underscore the importance of daily reflection in the literate lives of children. Phrases may include the following:

- "Wow! We did so much as writers today. This is your chance to name what you've learned."
- "Let's take a quiet moment and think about what we just did as writers this past hour and record it in our daybook."
- "I don't know about you, but sometimes I need to stop and think about how I'm feeling after I've done something important. Let's do that right now. Think quietly for one minute. Then, share your thoughts with a friend."

Just as Johnston acknowledges the importance of teachers considering the language they use in classrooms, it's important for children to do this same kind of reflective work as writers. Over time, this daily reflection compounds, creating cognizant writers who can describe what they know, what they still need to learn, how they feel about their progress, and how they measure up to other writers.

Monthly Reflections: Setting, Monitoring, and Meeting Goals

Each new genre study brings new possibilities of learning for writers. Memoirs give children the chance to tell stories about their lives. Informational reports offer writers opportunities to tell the world something they know that others might not. Book reviews can bring readers toward books that might hook them for life. How-tos can teach others a sequence for getting something done. Persuasive letters can change minds. Poetry presents possibilities for changing hearts. The writer starts fresh every couple of months—hits a reset button—and needs to reevaluate his or her writing goals for the promise of a new publication.

Setting, monitoring, and meeting goals require writers to reflect more specifically over a sustained amount of time. Writers feel agency when they commit these goals to paper and make a plan for achieving them. Combined with the reflective exercise of pondering ways to improve, writers empower themselves by scribing goals and visiting them often throughout a unit of study. Questions we want writers to consider include the following:

- *What do I want to be able to do as a writer in the next six to eight weeks? What is my goal?*
- *How am I going to make sure I achieve this goal?*
- *Who could help me achieve my goal? How can they help?*
- *When will I achieve this goal?*
- *If I do achieve this goal, what will it look like?*

At the beginning of each unit of study, writers *set* goals: they contemplate a new goal, talk about it with the teacher during a conference toward the beginning of a unit, and write it down (or have it recorded by the teacher) using a goals sheet (see appendix). These goals should be accessible to writers, so they might be glued into a daybook or three-hole-punched and put into a writer's folder.

Monthly, writers *monitor* their goals to make sure they are on target (see Figure 3.9). They revisit their goals sheets or engage in conversations with peers or teachers about the progress of their goals. Finally, at the end of the study, writers reflect on whether or not they *reached* the goals they set for themselves. They do this via contemplation and constant comparison. They determine whether they accomplished the mission they had for themselves as writers. Teachers can refer to these goals sheets occasionally in conference time to help students stretch their writing or focus on specific challenges they're facing.

Name: Emmie	Date: 9-22 15 Genre Unit of Study: Poetry

WRITE Goals

Writing Goals • Name your goal(s). •	• for people to under stand my poems. • Make long poems
Reaching Goals • Describe how you will reach your goal(s).	• Brainstorm bullets of ideas so I don't have to think before We write so don't spend all the time doing that. • Write about nature and look up things so I can do diffrent things about Nature.
Involving Others in Goals • Name others who might help you achieve your goal(s). • Describe *how* they might help.	• Mary can help me in frends poems. • Carsyn can help me learn about gym athleats • Carly, dance step and grace and buetie. • Mrs. Shut because She knows about notes and melidys
Timing of Goals • Set a date for when you intend to achieve this goal.	• christmas for presents • Halloween for my dog for her B-day. • Mums Birthday. • chrsitmas for santa
Evaluating Goals • Describe what it looks like when you successfully achieve your goal.	• books per gh etionle. • alot of smiles • happys and thank yous, • have a book.

Figure 3.9 A third grader sets goals for a poetry unit.

Digital Diversion: Capturing Reflections Digitally

The digital age allows us multimodal ways to capture reflective thinking. When we meet with students to confer about their goals or ask about artifacts they're choosing for a portfolio, we can bring digital devices. There are multiple ways to use phones or electronic tablets to capture students' voices:

Voice Memos: Most cell phones come with a free app that allows you to record your voice, download the recording, and send it via text message or e-mail. Instead of written reflections, writers can record a voiced reflection. Along with a photograph of the artifact, these voiced reflections can be uploaded to a student's web page or wiki page to create a multimodal portfolio that blends writing with speaking.

VoiceThread Writing Portfolios: VoiceThread is a digital tool that allows students to take photographs of artifacts and string those photographs together to create a gallery of student work. The tool allows students to describe the photograph displayed. Other VoiceThread users can access the students' gallery and leave video, voice, or text messages for the student. This makes the portfolio a more interactive experience for the writer and allows the writer to receive response from others.

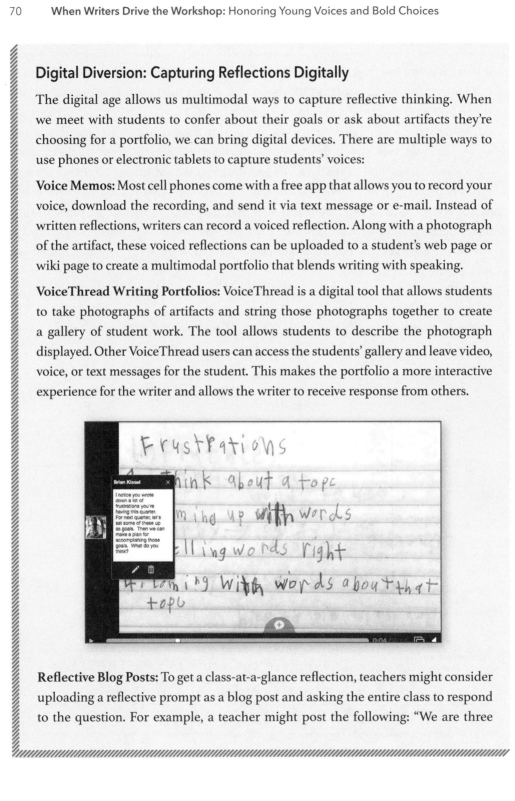

Reflective Blog Posts: To get a class-at-a-glance reflection, teachers might consider uploading a reflective prompt as a blog post and asking the entire class to respond to the question. For example, a teacher might post the following: "We are three weeks into our poetry study. What have you learned from our lessons about poetry so far? Please reflect on this question and post your response by Friday."

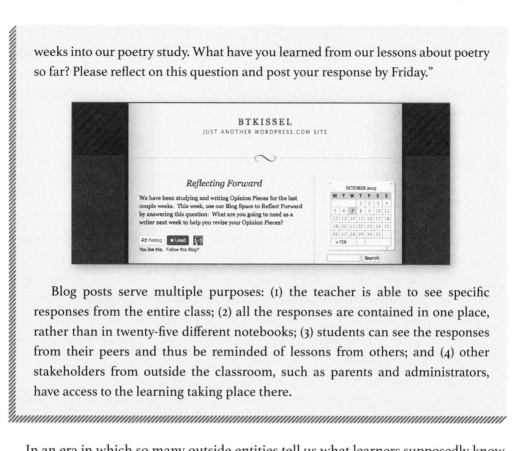

Blog posts serve multiple purposes: (1) the teacher is able to see specific responses from the entire class; (2) all the responses are contained in one place, rather than in twenty-five different notebooks; (3) students can see the responses from their peers and thus be reminded of lessons from others; and (4) other stakeholders from outside the classroom, such as parents and administrators, have access to the learning taking place there.

In an era in which so many outside entities tell us what learners supposedly know, wouldn't it be a novel exercise—maybe even an innovative one—for writers to reflect on their own learning and tell *us* what they know how to do?

Quarterly and Yearly Reflections: Portfolios

In a 2009 joint statement, the International Literacy Association and the National Council of Teachers of English declared the following: "Quality assessment is a process of inquiry. It requires gathering information and setting conditions so that the classroom, school, and community become centers of inquiry where students, teachers, and other stakeholders can examine their learning—individually and collaboratively—and find ways to improve their practice" (NCTE 2009). In this current era, how much voice do we give learners to describe their own learning?

We used to have spaces for learners to give voice to their literacy knowledge: portfolios. Portfolios are notebooks (with sheet protectors) or digital sites where students display artifacts to show what they have learned, over time, as writers. Some teachers still use portfolios to create a more balanced assessment system in their classrooms. Many more teachers can integrate them into their classrooms so that students have a voice at the assessment table.

Consider this example. Amy, a fourth grader, flips through her portfolio and displays the following:

- A photocopy of the cover of *Aunt Flossie's Hats (and Crab Cakes Later)* with a reflection about how Elizabeth Fitzgerald Howard, the author, uses flashbacks to tell the story. Amy explains how she emulated that same technique in her piece of writing about her dog.
- A draft of a memoir that is messy, long, and sometimes unfocused. But it shows that when she drafts, she writes faster than the little voice in her head that says, "This doesn't sound right. You need to stop writing."
- A draft that has been physically cut so she could see where she needs to add to a section, delete sections, and rearrange sections to show her revision process.
- A revised draft full of blue marks that shows verbs agreeing with subjects, added commas, crossed-out unnecessary words, and words spelled correctly after consulting a dictionary.
- A published piece of writing that shows her best work.
- A description of how her audience (mom and dad) responded to her published memoir (they cried because they were so proud).
- A photocopy of an anchor chart about developing characters that helped her make the characters in her memoir more three-dimensional.
- A photocopy of conference notes left by the teacher that encouraged her to consider a different beginning.
- A list of peers in the classroom who helped her revise her work and descriptions about how they helped.

What do we learn from writers through portfolio assessment? Amy's portfolio shows us that (1) authors influence her decisions, so she reads like a writer; (2) drafting isn't perfection, it's just getting it on the page; (3) revision means adding, deleting, and rearranging; (4) edits include correcting usage, punctuation, and spelling; (5) writers finish drafts by publishing them; (6) there is power in the reaction from intended audiences; (7) teachers can influence their students through powerful instruction; (8) conferring with others makes a difference; and (9) peers can give good advice.

In her book *When Learners Evaluate* (1998), Jane Hansen offers readers a self-evaluation process involving the following actions: collect, select, reflect, project, and affect; Figure 3.10 shows an anchor chart created with students to help them visualize the process. For writers putting together their portfolios, these actions manifest in the following ways:

- **Collect:** During designated times (for example, at the end of the quarter, halfway through the academic year, at the end of the year, or sometime in between), writers gather together the entirety of their writing lives: daybooks, notes, writing folders, drafts, revisions, edits, unfinished pieces, finished pieces, influential authors and their books, conference notes, and peer suggestions. They find a space in the classroom to spread out these materials. They collect the physical pieces of their writing and collect themselves psychologically to examine their work in an effort to name what they value about their learning.

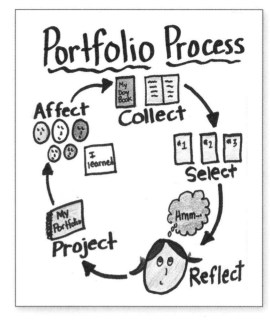

Figure 3.10 Anchor chart for a portfolio process

- **Select:** From the wide swath of materials, writers select artifacts that boldly reflect important learning moments. They are not restricted to final, completed products. They should also include artifacts that reveal their processes, their influences, and how others intervened in their learning. For each quarter, students should consider selecting three to five artifacts to include in their portfolios so that by the end of the school year, they have twelve to twenty artifacts to tell the story of their writing growth.
- **Reflect:** For each selection, students reflect on their choices. They thoughtfully examine their purpose for choosing each piece and what the artifact reveals about them as learners. The reflection portion of this process has its own subprocess in which writers do the following:

  - *Describe: What artifact did I choose?*
  - *Analyze: Why did I choose this artifact?*
  - *Appraise: What does this artifact show about me as a writer?*
  - *Influence: How can I use this artifact to teach others?*

Younger students might do these reflections verbally into a recording device or through dictation by the teacher. Older students write reflections to include with their artifacts.

Project: Writers project their learning for audiences. They may do this in an old-school way via binders with tabbed sections. Or, they may go digital by using a blog, wiki, or VoiceThread to project their learning (see "Digital Diversion" on page 70 for more). Just as published writing should be read by others, portfolios deserve a wide audience. Portfolio assessment, indeed, is a self-reflective endeavor for writers. But it's also a way to show other stakeholders (such as teachers, parents, and school administrators) what students know beyond what's tested. It's a counternarrative: *tests tell one story about me; let me offer you a fuller perspective.*

Frequently Asked Questions About Reflection

1. I'm already crunched for time. How am I going to add another couple of minutes to my workshop for reflection?

Ideally, writers reflect best if reflection happens directly after the author's chair. But time away can also give some perspective. Reflection can occur anytime throughout the day, including during transitions. You might consider posting a reflection question on your whiteboard or on an anchor chart and leaving it up throughout the day. That way, students can contemplate the question throughout the day (and across the curriculum) and respond to the reflection during those extra minutes in the morning, before and after lunch, and while settling in after recess or waiting for the bus in the afternoon.

2. I work with young children who are not yet writing conventionally. What other ways can I have them reflect besides via writing?

Teachers should consider the broad range of ways in which students reflect to include writing, speaking, listening, and visually representing. In addition to writing responses, students can reflect by

- turning and talking,
- speaking into a recorder app on a digital device,
- drawing responses, and
- engaging in whole-class discussions.

3. How would I do a whole-class discussion focused on reflection?

A couple of times a month, you might consider taking ten to fifteen minutes to engage in a Socratic discussion. You pose reflective questions, writers respond to them, and you record responses. Consider posing just three or four questions using the list of reflection questions on page 175 in the appendix. Your role is to pose questions. The children's role is to respond to those questions.

When I conduct these seminars, I stay out of the conversation as much as possible. Children, when they respond, look to me to get affirmation for their responses. I don't want them to think there are right and wrong answers to the questions I pose. So as students talk, I look down at my notes. That way, they stop looking toward me for affirmation and start talking more freely to one another.

4. *When you conduct reflection seminars, how do you document the responses?*

When I conduct seminars, I ask students to sit in a circle so they can all see one another. I draw the circle in my notebook and write the names of students around the circle. Then I pose the first question. Each time a student responds, I note it on my circle. Then I write quick, anecdotal notes capturing what each child says. I learn a lot from those notes:

- Who speaks and who doesn't speak. This can sometimes tell me about the personality of the child (extroverted versus introverted), the status of my classroom community (comfortable versus tense), and the reflective abilities of my students.
- What they say and what they do not say. When they speak, I get insight into their learning—and I can see which lessons and fellow writers have influenced them. I can also see possible misinterpretations that can be cleared up. I can learn just as much by what they don't say. This gives me some direction for future mini-lessons and conferences.
- How students build or don't build upon one another's responses. When students speak, I can monitor how well they listen to one another. I look for my seminars to maintain a flow, and I want writers to build upon the response of other writers. I can note this and offer future lessons about how we can build on the thinking of others in the classroom.

These discussions, and my notes from them, serve as powerful artifacts that show the quality of reflection happening within the classroom.

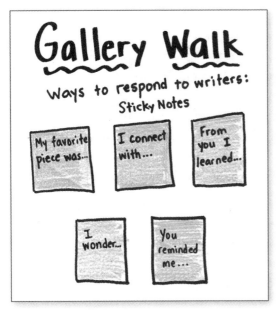

Figure 3.11 Anchor chart for gallery walk response

• **Affect:** As audiences read the portfolios of writers, writers should ask readers, "What have you learned *about* me? What have you learned *from* me? How are we connected as learners?" As audience members read the writers' portfolios, they can even leave responses (see Figure 3.11). In this way, portfolio assessment becomes dialectical. Students serve as teachers. Readers are affected by learning about others, learning from others, and discovering the connections that bind.

Travelogue

Personal reflection is difficult work. As we think back to the joys of life, we also confront the challenges. For every birth, marriage, and friendship we remember fondly, we may confront a death, divorce, or broken relationship. But when we refuse to reflect, we doom ourselves to repeat patterns in the future. It's the risk we take when we lead unreflective lives.

Writers suffer when their learning lacks reflection. It's crucial that we teachers make reflection a routine part of the day. Reflection for young writers is about examination for revelation. When writers reflect, they examine their writing lives and note strengths or acknowledge shortcomings. When writers reflect, they change behaviors because of their insights.

When writers reflect, they focus on awareness rather than achievement, contemplation rather than competition, individualization rather than standardization. For our children to learn about themselves as writers—and as people—they need time in contemplative reflection about their learning. Asking children to reflect on their learning—whether it's verbal or written—is much like asking someone to examine the joys and challenges of their lives. It begs writers to ask themselves, *Who am I? What am I projecting? How am I affecting others? What am I doing right? What skills do I need to refine?*

When children have answers to these questions, patterns emerge. Decisions become illumined. Young writers who reflect realize that their power to learn and grow does not come from the outside. Rather, it comes from within.

I interviewed a fifth grader named Rachel about her reflections. I asked her to go back into her daybook, find the various reflections she wrote, and offer a summary about what she noticed about herself as a writer. She made this powerful statement to me: "I care about what I'm writing. I have important things to say, and I'm saying them in my writing. I am a pretty good writer, and I think I'm getting better and better. I can learn more, and I will because I have a good teacher teaching me how to get better. I have friends who like to read my writing and give me feedback. I think I'm going to keep writing. Even in the summer—even when I don't have to write for school—I want to keep writing for myself."

Look how the pieces come together in the mosaic of Rachel's writing life. The outside edges of her writing life may have been formed from standardized testing data, but the inner pieces—those tiles that create the distinct, complete image and give the work its soul—are inlaid from the musings of a child who is reflective enough to find her voice. When writers drive the workshop, their reflections create a more fully formed portrait of who they are as learners.

Chapter 4

Mini-Lessons: Writers Determine the Detours

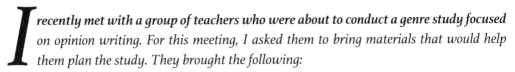

I *recently met with a group of teachers who were about to conduct a genre study focused on opinion writing. For this meeting, I asked them to bring materials that would help them plan the study. They brought the following:*

- *a unit of study on opinion writing from a packaged program purchased by the school*
- *a notebook of opinion lessons downloaded from a website of teacher resources*
- *ideas from Pinterest*
- *a curriculum map from the district office*
- *lesson plans from the previous year*

Teachers began planning. They took a blank calendar, opened the packaged program, and plotted out lessons for Day 1, Day 2, Day 3, and so forth. After fifteen minutes, I asked them to do a quick-write reflection using the following question: "Where are our students' voices in the planning process for this unit of study?"

Teachers reflected, wrote, and shared their thoughts with colleagues. Amy's reflection struck a chord with the group:

"As we were planning this unit, something didn't feel right to me. I felt like I was planning a vacation for my family but I was making all the decisions about what to do. I set the schedule. I picked the restaurants. I determined our excursions. Is that what I'm doing here as a teacher? I know there are things I must teach. But shouldn't I be thinking about my students in this process, too? It's like I need to think about my last family vacation and ask, What worked? What didn't work? And what kind of vacation can I plan that's responsive to my family?*"*

Amy's teammates nodded. They affirmed her thinking. Another teammate offered her reflection: "I asked, What's missing from this table? *I need conference notes about my kids. I need to know what they know and don't know. My students' voices aren't present today because I didn't bring their voices to the table.*"

The teachers went back to their classrooms and returned five minutes later with their conference notebooks. They began poring over their notes to discover what students knew, what students were learning, and what they still needed to learn. Their notes joined the other materials on the table.

This is what happens when students, not packaged programs or cute graphic organizers from a website, guide instruction. Students are the center of instruction. By carefully analyzing what they've done as learners, we help them reclaim the instructional agenda.

Planning with Students in Mind

In most books about the writer's workshop, a chapter about mini-lessons appears somewhere toward the beginning. So it might seem that this chapter in misplaced. It's not.

I think it's unwise for teachers to make too many whole-class instructional decisions before they've had time to confer, listen to young writers in the author's chair, and analyze what students have learned so far from their reflections. It's important for us to map out big ideas: a yearly plan of genre study; general lessons to teach within each genre; ideas to generate purposes, audiences, and ideas for a unit of study; and due dates for the end units. But the magic of instruction unfurls as students are entrenched in their writing processes and we hear about their struggles and triumphs. Teachers guide writers toward the destination, but writers take us on important detours along the way (see the following sidebar).

Guiding Beliefs About Mini-Lessons

The following beliefs reveal my understanding of mini-lessons. These beliefs guide my practice in classrooms and keep me focused on the purpose for each mini-lesson:

1. Writers and their teacher negotiate the types of mini-lessons needed.

In a given genre study, many packaged curricula determine the mini-lessons that should be taught and the sequence in which they unfold in a workshop. In a student-driven workshop, teachers plan mini-lessons that combine the demands of the genre with the moves writers make as the genre study unfolds. Therefore, planning mini-lessons becomes a negotiated process between the teacher and his or her writers. The teacher brings forward lessons that help writers understand the genre. Writers show the teacher which procedural, process, and skills lessons they still need to be effective authors.

2. Mini-lessons are co-taught by teachers and students.

Teachers guide most mini-lessons—particularly genre mini-lessons focused on text structures and text features. However, as they pay close attention to what writers do as they construct within a genre, many of the interesting moves writers make offer powerful lessons for the entire class. If we believe in a student-centered workshop, then students should be co-teachers for several lessons.

3. Writers determine which mini-lesson strategies to weave into their writing.

Mini-lessons present opportunities for our writers—not dictates. When we teach a lesson to writers, we offer options that they may or may not weave into their writing. In student-led workshops, writers choose the mini-lessons that are most applicable to their writing. They may choose to embed the mini-lesson into their writing the same day the mini-lesson lesson is taught, months later, or never.

4. In writer-driven workshops, planning happens daily and weekly.

If we are being responsive to the needs of our writers, then planning for writing happens daily and weekly—not quarterly. We may create a road map for instruction, but the road map needs to be flexible. As we confer with writers, patterns emerge that tell us unexpected areas to address. When this happens, we take detours from our plan and address them.

5. Planning for writing involves analysis of our anecdotal writing records.

Because planning requires careful study of the writers within our classrooms, people from outside our classrooms should not plan the instruction. We must resist the urge to have one teacher from a grade level plan instruction for all teachers across the grade level. Effective grade-level planning combines discussion about a genre, study of that genre as a team, and analysis of conference notes and student writing to determine daily and weekly lessons. All teachers must plan for writing—and we start the planning by first focusing on our writers.

Negotiations in the Planning Process

When planning a new genre study, several elements coalesce to build the road map of instruction (see Figure 4.1). First, we look back at our notes (conference notes, author's chair notes, reflection notes) and analyze them. We ask, *What have my students learned? What do they still need to learn?* Those notes provide important guidance about lessons that need to be woven into what they need to learn next. As we conduct a genre study, writers make discoveries about mentor authors that they capture in their daybooks or we capture on an anchor chart. We consider exploring those discoveries in more depth as we plan instruction. Next, we consider the elements of the genre that distinguish it from other genres. We wonder, *What do our students need to know to write within this genre?* Finally, we examine the standards our state asks us to address and, if applicable, a district-mandated program or writing curriculum. Often, what our students need as writers matches the demands of the state standards and mandated programs. But sometimes they diverge. This divergence provides opportunity for instruction.

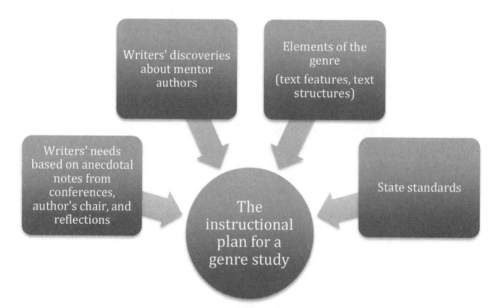

Figure 4.1 Components of an instructional plan for a genre study

To illustrate this point: recently, my wife, Hattie, and I took our children to the Bechtler Museum of Modern Art in Charlotte, North Carolina. Hattie majored in art history in college and worked as an arts educator for a museum. She knows how to make you fall in love with art! It's important to her that our children have the same appreciation, so for our visit, she packed their backpacks with drawing pads and colored pencils. When we got to the museum, the kids received a scavenger hunt sheet that encouraged them to search for the museum's notable works.

There was a series of must-sees throughout the museum: the Picasso drawing, the Jasper Johns panel, the Degas pastel, and the Warhol silk screens. Hattie explained the artwork in a way that made sense to two seven-year-olds and a five-year-old by providing interesting tidbits about the artists to keep the children engaged. Then the children roamed the museum to make their own discoveries. Charlie sat in front of a Victor Vasarely painting—a work of blue, purple, red, and green geometric boxes on canvas—and started mimicking the work in his notebook. Ben found a fascinating brass sculpture by Günter Haese and started sketching a pencil version of it in his notebook. Harriet stopped at a whimsical Alexander Calder mobile and re-created it in her notebook. All three were drawn to a different artist and a different medium beyond our own must-see list. And, because they stopped for a bit to study it, Hattie and I stopped for a bit to discover it with them.

This is similar to how we should see our instructional planning as writing teachers. Through a series of mini-lessons, we take our students to the must-sees of a genre study—the text features of informational writing, the various structures of narrative writing, the evidence that supports persuasive writing, or the stanzas that make poetry sing. We make sure we cover the key works—the standards—because we are expected to know them to build our knowledge. But along the way, our students will make their own discoveries. And those discoveries are just as important! So, we need to pay attention. We must stop and ponder alongside them when we confer. It's through the conferring lens that we learn about our students—about what they know, what captures their attention, and what confuses them.

Teachers and learners negotiate the planning process. You have specific lessons and skills you need to bring forward. Students bring specific needs or goals from previous studies. All these needs coalesce in a responsive instructional plan that continues to be renegotiated throughout the year.

A Planning Process Responsive to Student Needs

Teachers spend the first several weeks of school laying the foundation for writer's workshop success. We ask ourselves, *How do I want this classroom to function during writing? How do I want students to respond to one another? How can I create a space for students to feel safe, secure, and productive?*

Students bring their own set of questions: *Why am I writing in this classroom? Will*

I have a teacher this year who will allow me to choose my topics, audiences, purposes? Will I share my writing with others? Will this be a safe place for me as a writer? The first few weeks focus on habits, routines, and trust.

Then, writing begins.

The most effective way to plan instruction is similar to the way students learn about a genre—through an inquiry process. Figure 4.2 illustrates the planning process, which goes something like this:

- **Gather resources**, with the understanding that the most important resource is the notes you have written about your students as writers.
- **Ask questions** that lead your own inquiry into the genre.
- **Study** students and elements of the genre. Find mentor authors to serve as co-teachers as well.
- **Create** sample texts and lessons.
- **Teach** lessons and allow students to lead where you go next.
- **Reflect** on the notes you take, and adjust instruction accordingly.

Figure 4.2 A teacher's planning process

Once routines and habits are established, we introduce genre study to our students. Every six to eight weeks, we plan to focus on teaching a specific genre that will culminate in at least one published piece for a purpose and audience decided upon by the writer. Writers might draft several pieces, but they are responsible for publishing at least one piece during the six-to-eight-week study.

I say this cautiously—fearing it could be interpreted as students writing *only* within one genre for six to eight weeks. If we believe choice is a foundational condition of writing, then genre choice must be an option as well. Thus begins another negotiation. I typically say something like this: "For the next two months, I'm going to focus our mini-lessons on persuasive writing. By the end of the two months, I expect you to have a finished persuasive piece—one that has an authentic purpose and audience for you. I want you to write within this genre so you can learn about new genre possibilities. You might even fall in love with this new genre and want to write in it all the time! It's my job to show you these possibilities. But that does not mean you are limited to writing persuasive pieces for the next two months. Continue pursuing your own writing interests. Just make sure that at the end of these two months, one of your published pieces is a persuasive one."

Once we determine which genre will be the focus, we gather resources.

Gather Resources

Blank spaces provide fresh opportunities. We plan for teaching a genre by tossing a variety of materials on an empty table and cluttering the space with possibilities. Our tables fill with notes about students, mentor texts, lessons from the previous year, and district guides, and soon we're overwhelmed with the heft of competing items:

- **Resources about our students:** conference notes, author's chair notes, reflection notes, goals sheets, and portfolios
- **Resources by teachers:** teacher writing from past years, effective lessons taught in the past, anchor charts, daybook handouts from previous years
- **Resources from the school district:** curriculum guides, state standards
- **Resources from outside the district:** mentor texts, packaged curricula (to glean ideas), and Internet resources

The resources are stacked high like instructional skyscrapers. We sift, sort, and prioritize from possibilities. We ask, "For the next six to eight weeks, what do the majority of students need to learn?" And from each stack we pause and ponder. Questions arise.

Ask Questions

If we want students to approach writing from an inquiry stance, then we must inquire ourselves when we plan instruction. A lack of inquiry is the most frustrating part of prescribed, packaged curricula. When we are given scripts, we're not allowed to question—and neither are our writers. A dangerous cycle begins: no questioning leads to no reflection, which leads to unchallenged thinking. We want deeper thinking that leads to deeper writing. Inquiry is the key.

We approach each genre study with different sets of questions. Because students drive instruction, we inquire about them first. Questions based on *student resources* might include the following:

- By scanning conference notes: *What do most of my students know how to do? What do they not know how to do yet?*
- By scanning author's chair notes: *Who is responding to the author? Who isn't responding? How is the quality of response? Why might this be happening?*
- By scanning reflection quick-writes: *What have my students learned? How do they see themselves as writers? What do they want to know now?*
- By scanning goals sheets from the previous study: *Did the majority of students meet their goals? If not, why? What are their goals for this genre study?*
- By scanning portfolios: *What are my students valuing as writers? What else do I think they should value?*

Next, we teachers look within to examine ourselves as writers. We ask questions that focus on our own experiences crafting writing within this genre and think about what we already know or don't know based on our own experiences. Questions based on *teacher* resources might include these:

- *Have I ever written anything within this genre?*
- *When I've written in this genre myself, what has been tricky?*
- *If I were to write a sample text within this genre, what would I need to include so my students include it, too?*
- *Have I collected any samples of this genre from past years? If not (or if I'm a new teacher), is there a colleague who has?*
- *What are some of my favorite lessons from the past that I could use again this year?*
- *Because I don't want everyone to write in the same way, in what ways might I write within this genre to reflect the diversity of structures that are possible?*

States and school districts have expectations about what our students must know about writing at various grade levels. We examine *state and school district standards* and ask another round of questions:

- *What skills and concepts is the state requiring me to teach for this genre? What mini-lessons could I prepare to teach them?*
- *What are the grade-level expectations for this genre?*

- *Are there state-mandated assessments attached to this genre? If so, what do I need to consider for students to be successful on that assessment?*
- *Do I see my students within these standards? That is, which standards are appropriate for my students? Do some writers need me to address standards from grade levels above or below?*
- *What's missing from the standards that I still think is important to teach?*

Finally, we look at the pile of resources that come from a variety of places. We delve into these materials and inquire. Questions that might arise based on *resources from outside the classroom* include these:

- *Who are known authors in this genre?*
- *Have I collected books that reflect diversity (diverse authors, diverse characters, diverse settings, diverse topics, diverse interests)?*
- *Have I collected examples that represent a variety of formats (digital formats, videos, magazines, newspapers, and so on)?*
- *When my students study narrative and poetry (including memoir), will they see people who look like them in many of the books? Will they see people who don't look like them in many of the books so they can learn about others?*
- *When collecting informational and persuasive texts, did I include texts on topics that will engage my students?*
- *Did I find texts that include varied text structures: narrative (flashback, beginning-middle-end, no-time, and so on), informational (description, sequence, problem-solution, cause-effect, and compare/contrast), poetry (syllable- and word-count poems, free verse, rhyming verse, concrete, and so on)?*

We use these questions as a guide for study. And as we study, we begin to determine the lessons our writers need.

Study

Teaching can be an isolating profession, and many teachers find themselves studying their students in isolation. If you're like me, you get much-needed energy from a focused, engaged collaboration with colleagues. I spent time recently in a school that designed grade-level meetings as inquiry meetings—putting the housekeeping issues in an easy-to-read e-mail so the majority of meeting time could be spent discussing pedagogy. Each time teachers left their grade-level meetings, they felt energized rather than drained. Those meetings often involved grade-level teams studying the conference notes they took about their writers.

Studying Conference Notes for Whole-Class Lessons

In a student-driven workshop, conference notes are the engines of instruction. We record notes to chart the progress of individual writers and to see a compass direction pointing toward one-on-one or small-group differentiated instruction. But as we examine the notes across a classroom of students, patterns emerge that become our map to whole-class mini-lessons.

At the beginning of a new genre study, we should take some time to re-analyze our notes and wonder, *What are the processes and skills writers are grasping? What are the processes and skills I need to revisit in instruction?* Consider creating a chart of processes and skills you want to teach in the next study and, as you skim past conference notes, mark the chart with tally marks denoting successes and struggles (see Figure 4.3). This analysis can be done quickly and instinctively. Our purpose is not precision—our purpose is recording possibilities for potential lessons. When the chart is completed, patterns emerge and inform instruction. We learn where we should linger and when to move onward.

Studying Conference Notes to Find Student Co-Teachers

In classrooms where students drive the curriculum, young writers will write in unexpected, fascinating ways. When this happens, take notice and bring the writers forward to teach the class something new. These are unplanned moments—moments that are never found in curriculum guides or packaged programs. For example, I once worked in a kindergarten classroom with a young writer who was fascinated with pop-up books. In an effort to create his own, he figured out a way to fold paper and glue it into his booklet so his illustrations would pop up whenever a reader turned the page.

I asked the boy to drive the next day's mini-lesson. Standing in front of his peers, he placed his book under the document camera and explained how he had created it. He told his peers about the pop-up books he had at home and said he wanted to create his own because he knew other children would love reading them. His peers, captivated, clapped when he finished teaching. For several weeks, pop-up books were a popular format in the classroom.

There are many teachers in student-driven writing classrooms, and they're not all standing in front of the room. When we notice the interesting things students do, praise their ingenuity, and bring their craft to the attention of the entire class, learners become teachers. Teaching voices emerge.

Previous Genre Study Research-Based Report Writing (Fifth Grade)

	STUDENTS WERE *SUCCESSFUL* WITH THIS DURING THE PREVIOUS GENRE STUDY	STUDENTS *STRUGGLED* WITH THIS DURING THE PREVIOUS GENRE STUDY
PROCESS		
Brainstorming ideas for a topic	✓✓✓✓✓✓✓✓ ✓✓✓✓✓	✓✓✓✓
Planning	✓✓	✓✓✓✓✓✓✓✓✓ ✓✓✓✓✓✓✓
Conducting research	✓	✓✓✓✓✓✓✓✓✓ ✓✓✓✓✓✓✓✓
Searching online for information	✓✓	✓✓✓✓✓✓✓✓✓✓ ✓✓✓✓✓✓✓
Drafting	✓✓✓✓✓✓✓✓ ✓✓✓✓✓✓✓✓✓	✓✓
Revising beginnings	✓✓✓✓✓✓✓✓✓ ✓✓✓✓✓✓	✓✓✓✓
Revising endings	✓✓✓✓✓✓✓✓✓	✓✓✓✓✓✓✓✓✓
Staying focused on one topic or story line	✓✓✓✓✓	✓✓✓✓✓✓✓✓✓✓ ✓✓✓✓✓
Elaborating	✓✓	✓✓✓✓✓✓✓✓✓ ✓✓✓✓✓✓✓
Using transitional words	✓✓✓✓✓✓✓✓ ✓✓✓✓✓✓✓✓	✓✓
Organizing the writing	✓✓✓✓✓✓✓✓✓ ✓✓✓✓✓✓✓✓	✓
Publishing	✓✓✓✓✓✓✓✓ ✓✓✓✓✓✓✓✓✓	✓✓
SKILLS		
Using commas in a series	✓✓✓✓✓✓✓✓ ✓✓✓✓✓✓✓✓✓	✓✓
Using commas to separate an introductory clause	✓✓✓✓✓	✓✓✓✓✓✓✓✓✓ ✓✓✓✓✓
Correctly recognizing shifts in verb tense	✓✓✓✓✓✓✓✓✓ ✓✓✓✓✓✓	✓✓✓✓

Figure 4.3 Studying and marking conference notes

Studying Author's Chair Notes

The notes we take during author's chair sessions also provide fresh data about our students as writers and responders. When we scan these notes we notice the following:

- The types of response authors seek
- The kind of feedback the audience provides
- Who offers feedback and who doesn't
- The quality of the feedback

Again we look for patterns rather than precision. And, because writer's workshop is part of an overall language arts curriculum, our analysis is not confined to writing—we should also study how children speak and listen. We can take our author's chair notes and write a five-to-six-minute quick-write about what we see (Figure 4.4).

Author's Chair Analysis
Time Period: From October 15 to December 1

TYPES OF RESPONSE	HOW DO PEERS RESPOND?
I notice a lot of writers seeking compliments. Even when they are revising their work, it seems like a lot of writers want the validation. I wonder: are they not feeling confident? I wonder why they aren't seeking more suggestions. Maybe they are fearful of the feedback.	The class is responding with compliments, but it feels like the compliments are a bit on the surface level. Authors are getting a lot of "You added lots of details." But they are not being specific enough with the quality of detail and why those details supported them as readers.
WHO OFFERED FEEDBACK?	**WHO DIDN'T OFFER FEEDBACK?**
Jack and Amber are offering tons of feedback to writers. Their hands always shoot up to respond. Ben is always willing to respond, but he's rarely called upon. Why?	I never see Amy offering feedback. Chaz looks elsewhere when an author shares. Is he present as a listener?
WHAT IS THE QUALITY OF THE FEEDBACK?	**POSSIBLE MINI-LESSONS TO TEACH**
For the most part, listeners are responding to the author's agenda. When they offer compliments, I feel like they could be richer—more in-depth. I need to model this! What does it mean to have "good details"?	• Asking for different types of response • Calling on different voices to offer feedback • Listening to the author • Facing the author and giving the author your attention

Figure 4.4 Author's Chair Analysis notes

Studying Reflection Notes and Self-Evaluations

We can reserve three to four mini-lessons during each study to engage in Socratic seminars based on students' self-reflections. Instead of a formal lesson, we talk. In Socratic seminars, teachers pose questions. Students initiate the conversation and make sure it continues in respectful ways. To prepare for these seminars, teachers scan students' self-reflections, goals sheets, and portfolios in search of questions to pose to the group. There are many possibilities, but Figure 4.5 offers some guidance:

TYPE OF REFLECTION	WHAT I SEE IN STUDENTS' REFLECTIONS	POSSIBLE SOCRATIC SEMINAR QUESTIONS
Quick-write questions focused on looking back	• Some students admit to goofing off and wasting time. • Some students did just what we discussed in the mini-lesson. • Some students continued with previous work. • Some students worked with peers.	• How are you spending your time writing in this class?
Goals sheets	• Goals focus primarily on spelling words and mechanics. • Many students didn't know what goals to set for themselves.	• Many of you noted that becoming a better speller is an important goal of yours. Why is this an important goal? • What ideas might we have about other goals we can set for ourselves for this genre study?
Portfolios	• Children picked artifacts that showed how various lessons crept into their finished products. • Children picked influential authors who helped them write within the genre.	• What did you learn about yourself as a writer during this genre study?

Figure 4.5 Studying reflection notes to prepare for a Socratic seminar

Most important, the questions we pose shouldn't be arbitrary and prescribed. For the Socratic seminar to feel authentic, the questions posed should come from the contemplative study of reflection artifacts.

Studying Mentor Authors

Perhaps the most time-consuming part of studying comes when we search, read, and analyze the published writing of mentor authors. Much decision making takes place to

find authors to help co-teach our lessons. If we're asking mentor authors to sit alongside us to teach students about writing, their work needs to be worth our instructional
time. I search for authors who

- have an interesting point of view;
- write with a strong voice;
- write in a way that engages young readers;
- write about diverse characters, settings, and topics;
- produce some texts that align with the reading level of most students in my
  classroom;
- write strong beginnings and endings;
- use precise nouns and verbs so their writing is not cluttered with unnecessary
  adjectives and adverbs;
- display clear text structures; and
- inspire young writers with their creativity and ingenuity.

Time, and lack of it, tempts us to just use what we've found on someone's Pinterest
board or in our Twitter feed. Honestly, sometimes I start there. But if we continue to
use the same books, from the same authors, year after year, how are we any different
from the prescribed curricula we're trying to resist? New authors emerge every day, and
they have compelling things to say through their writing. Authors of color, who bring
forward diverse characters and important perspectives, publish books every year that
need to find their ways into our classrooms. Familiarize yourself with booklists and
award winners from the American Library Association and the International Literacy
Association, follow favorite authors on Goodreads, and participate in popular Twitter
chats such as #TitleTalk. Make friends with your school or community librarian, too,
and ask for recommendations. You can't read every single children's book, but certainly
you can find new and interesting mentor texts for your students each year.

Strong writers are well-read readers. Strong writing teachers are well-read readers
of children's literature. A thoughtful way to spend the first week or so of a genre study
is to do no writing at all. Instead, the class (including the teacher) spends the entire
workshop time engaged in reading. We read texts as writers—studying the thoughtful
moves an author made to construct a compelling text.

We can even narrow our reading focus. For younger children, we can do this as a
whole class during read-aloud. After reading a text aloud, we might revisit it and analyze it in specific ways. We might even chart what we notice so students can use this as
a guide in their own writing (see Figure 4.6). For older students, this work can be done
in groups: one group analyzes how authors begin and end their texts, another group

Mentor Authors
Craft Focus: Text Structures of Memoirs

TEXT/AUTHOR	DIRECT FROM THE TEXT	RECOMMENDED TO USE FOR A WHOLE-CLASS MINI-LESSON	
Two Mrs. Gibsons By Toyomi Igus Narrative Text Structure: Compare and Contrast	I once knew two Mrs. Gibsons (1). This Mrs. Gibson was tall. Her skin was the color of chocolate. She was born in America in a place called Tennessee. This Mrs. Gibson was small. Her skin was the color of vanilla. She was born in Japan in a place called Gifu (2).	Yes	No
When I Was Young in the Mountains By Cynthia Rylant Narrative Text Structure: No-Time Narrative (Fletcher 2007)	When I was young in the mountains, Grandfather came home in the evening covered with the black dust of a coal mine. Only his lips were clean, and he used them to kiss the top of my head (1). When I was young in the mountains… When I was young in the mountains…	Yes	No
Aunt Flossie's Hats (And Crab Cakes Later) By Elizabeth Fitzgerald Howard Narrative Text Structure: Flashback	One Sunday afternoon, I picked out a wooly winter hat, sort of green, maybe. Aunt Flossie thought a minute. Aunt Flossie almost always thinks a minute before she starts a hat story. Then she sniffed the wooly hat (31).	Yes	No

Figure 4.6 Studying mentor authors

analyzes structure, another searches for creative uses of words, and another looks at inventive ways of using text features. Then we come together to share what we learned.

The study of mentor authors should be a shared exercise. Young children often find elements within a text that we miss entirely. In this process where we gather, ask, study, create, ask again, teach, and reflect, the act of studying has a prominent role throughout.

Create Sample Texts and Lessons

Studying leads our creative process. After we discover what our writers know (and don't know yet), features of a new genre, and grade-level expectations, we can begin creating the tools we need to teach the genre. In this stage of a teacher's planning process, we can create texts to immerse ourselves in the genre and then create lessons to help guide the genre study.

Creating Sample Texts

It's not enough for us to study texts authors compose. We need to compose texts ourselves. When we compose texts, we get insider access to the genre. And we develop a sense of what our students go through when they compose texts.

Creating texts requires nuance. In one sense, we want to create texts with predictable structures for students to emulate. But there's danger in composing texts as *the* model for students to follow. For any given genre, there are *many* possibilities a student should use to derive structural guidance. Our own compositions should reflect that diversity.

I've spent this past year teaching writing in my son's first-grade classroom. As I prepared to teach informational writing, I wanted insight into the genre by composing informational texts to use as demonstrations.

This was the composing process I used to create my text:

- **Research:** Based on what I knew about the students after asking questions and studying notes as described in the above sections, I knew my sample text(s) should contain the following:

  - *A clear topic*
  - *A structure (sequence, description, cause/effect, problem/solution, compare/contrast)*
  - *Facts*
  - *Some sort of beginning or introduction*
  - *Some sort of closure*
  - *Illustrations that might incorporate various text features*
  - *Spelling at a letter-name stage of spelling development (that is, words that are spelled out by using sounds, but that may have errors in the vowel patterns within the words)*
  - *Capital letters at the beginning of sentences and punctuation at the end*

- **Brainstorming:** It was important for the topics to be universal and relatable to first graders, but it also had to be about a topic I knew something about. I brainstormed a list of topics and matched my list to the five most common informational text structures:

- *Sequence (how-to): how to make a healthful lunch, how to play tennis, how to juggle, how to take care of a dog*
- *Description (all-about books): dogs, soccer, dollywood, fish*
- *Compare/contrast: dogs and cats, country music and pop music, math and reading*
- *Cause and effect: pollution in the ocean*
- *Problem and solution: fighting with friends, getting ready for school, homework*

- **Deciding:** I scanned the potential topics and determined which ones would be best to use. For the first graders, I decided to create three sample texts focused on sequence, description, and comparing and contrasting. I decided not to teach cause and effect or problem and solution, because my time was limited and those structures are a bit more complicated—developmentally, they may be more applicable for a later grade. However, I wasn't closed to the possibility and decided I might touch upon those structures later when I conferred individually with students. Also, because students guide the instruction, I knew I might decide to include those structures later.

I also needed to decide how my mentor text(s) would appear on the page. I had choices: (1) write a draft and use the draft to revise and edit in front of the students, (2) create a fully developed, published text so students could see what my final product looked like, (3) compose a text free from any grammatical and spelling errors, or (4) leave some errors in the sample so it would look similar to the work of the students. So many choices! That is why we shouldn't limit ourselves to *one* mentor text. When we offer a variety of model texts, we (and our students) are not trapped within a restrictive rhetorical box.

- **Writing:** I went through my own process for constructing the text and discovered that my process is recursive—a blend of planning, drafting, revising, and editing that is different every time I compose something new. When we write ourselves, we quickly learn that our young writers engage in their *own* writing processes—it changes from writer to writer, piece of writing to piece of writing. We don't understand this until we ourselves compose. When we do, the posters that inaccurately displayed *the* writing process as a sequence of steps usually come off our walls. Because there's no such thing as *the* writing process. When we accept that everyone engages in his or her *own* process, then we're okay if, within a classroom of writers, some are brainstorming, some are planning, some are drafting, some are revising, some are editing, some are illustrating, some are recording, and some are publishing. In classrooms where writers drive, they also drive their writing process (see Figure 4.7).

Dollywood

Written and Illustrated by:
Brian Kissel

Many families go to Dollywood for their family vacation.

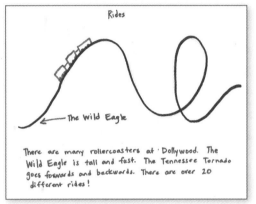

Rides

The Wild Eagle

There are many rollercoasters at Dollywood. The Wild Eagle is tall and fast. The Tennessee Tornado goes forwards and backwards. There are over 20 different rides!

Shows

Dollywood has lots of fun shows to watch. You can listen to music at some shows. You can pop bubbles at the Million Bubble show. There are shows for everyone to enjoy.

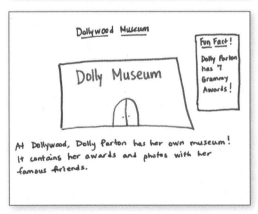

Dollywood Museum

Dolly Museum

Fun Fact!
Dolly Parton has 7 Grammy Awards!

At Dollywood, Dolly Parton has her own museum! It contains her awards and photos with her famous friends.

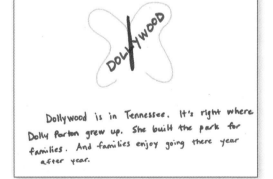

DOLLYWOOD

Dollywood is in Tennessee. It's right where Dolly Parton grew up. She built the park for families. And families enjoy going there year after year.

Figure 4.7 A teacher-created informational text for first grade

- **Displaying:** Finally, I decided how I would display my writing. First, I made an anchor chart because I wanted my writing to be a permanent fixture on the walls. That way I could go back, refer to it, and revise it along the way. Next, I made half-sheet photocopies of my writing so every child had a copy for his or her daybook. This allowed them to access my writing when they needed it. It also allowed us to dissect it—drawing arrows to beginnings, circling unique words, making edits, noting structures, and examining text features.

Our teacher-created texts serve multiple purposes. At the surface level, they provide models for our young writers who need examples to help them see possibilities. At a deeper level, they immerse teachers in our own writing process. Can we really teach writing effectively if we never engage in writing ourselves? How do we know what to say to children if we are not insiders to the genre? And how do we gain the empathy needed for the child who struggles as a writer if we have never faced similar struggles ourselves? If we want students to drive the writer's workshop, we must be in tune with the real feelings and struggles our young writers experience—and we do this by creating our own texts.

Creating Lessons

When planning for whole-class instruction, we're deciding which mini-lessons to teach and when. But if we're being responsive to what our students are doing as writers, *what* we teach during our mini-lessons sometimes changes and *when* we teach those mini-lessons changes often.

What we teach is an amalgam of different types of lessons that include the following:

- **Procedural Mini-Lessons:** These are lessons that address *how* we do things in this classroom so we can write. They cover anything from how to sit during the mini-lesson to how to respond in the author's chair to how to be respectful during writing groups. Procedural mini-lessons are heavy at the beginning of the year but make occasional appearances throughout the year when new procedures (or annoyances) emerge. These lessons are student driven, and we teach them based on what we notice our students doing in the workshop.

- **Process Mini-Lessons:** These lessons address the processes we go through to construct texts. Process mini-lessons include determining author and purpose for our work, brainstorming ideas, drafting, revising, and publishing. No matter the genre, we repeatedly teach these processes over and over again throughout the year. These lessons are sometimes student driven, sometimes teacher driven. We pay attention to what our students do while in the process of writing. If they need additional lessons on brainstorming ideas, we build in additional lessons.

- **Skills Mini-Lessons:** These lessons focus on editing. For skills mini-lessons, I consult state standards at the grade level and skim the standards at the preceding grade (for writers who have not yet mastered skills taught earlier) and the next grade (for writers ready to move forward). These lessons focus on usage, punctuation, and spelling patterns, and they tend to be district or state driven—ideally based on developmental appropriateness, although, unfortunately, that is not always the case.

- **Genre Mini-Lessons:** These lessons specifically address elements of the genre. Genre mini-lessons are genre dependent, and teachers can plan them in advance because they are genre driven. For these lessons we can study our curriculum guides and curricular resources we may have around the school, and can even get ideas online to support our instruction.

For any given six-to-eight-week genre study, there's an opportunity to teach a mini-lesson four or five days a week. Typically, the majority of mini-lessons focus on process and genre, so consider planning for the lessons to unfold as shown in Figure 4.8.

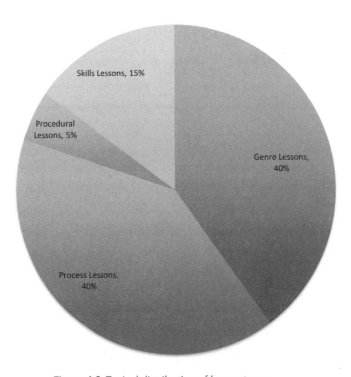

Figure 4.8 Typical distribution of lesson types

Teach

When we teach various lessons depends on our writers. In my early teaching life, I pulled out a calendar and placed lessons on specific days—it was a fixed way of planning in which I viewed lessons as placeholders for the days of the week. I thought, *This is what I will teach on Monday, Tuesday, Wednesday, Thursday, and Friday.*

But as I started weaving in the knowledge I gained from paying attention to students, I realized that this way of thinking was unresponsive to their needs. Instead of placing mini-lessons on a calendar, I think of lessons as items on an instructional menu (see Figure 4.9). I have a collection of lessons ready to go for the genre study. But because I now pay closer attention to what writers are doing, I'm flexible about *when* I teach those lessons.

PROCEDURAL MINI-LESSONS	SKILL	PROCESS	GENRE

• **New Procedural Lesson:** Engaging in writing groups
• **Revisit Procedural Lesson:** What to do when a writer completes a draft
• **Revisit Procedural Lesson:** Responding to writers
• **New Procedural Lesson:** Celebrating informational texts by seeking online feedback
	• **New Skill Lesson:** Using commas to separate words such as *Yes* and *No*
	• **Revisit Skill Lesson:** Using commas when writing in a series
	• **Revisit Skill Lesson:** Using a comma to separate an introductory clause
		• **New Process Lesson:** Planning and using a graphic organizer for research-based informational reports
		• **New Process Lesson:** Revising for organization of informational writing
		• **Revisit Drafting Lesson:** Drafting multiple informational topics so we have choices
		• **New Process Lesson:** Revising for words
		• **New Process Lesson:** Revising for voice in informational text
		• **New Process Lesson:** Publishing an informational text digitally
			• How to conduct research on the Internet
			• Beginnings of informational reports
			• Endings of informational reports
			• Multiple text structures
			  ▪ Text features
			  ▪ Diagrams
			  ▪ Maps
			  ▪ Charts
			  ▪ Headings
			  ▪ Subheadings

Figure 4.9 An instructional menu of lessons

From the collection of notes we compile from studying, an instructional vision emerges. We begin to see the lessons we must teach to help students write within the genre. And we can start to create a menu that combines lessons that will be new to students with lessons we revisit based on what we discovered by studying our notes.

If you're a member of AAA, you might have heard of TripTiks. You can contact AAA and tell them where you're driving for your next trip, and they will prepare a booklet of maps that provide a route to get from Point A to Point B. My family gets one when we drive to visit relatives in Florida. Sure, I know we can use Google Maps on our smartphones, but we prefer the printed version. There's great satisfaction in flipping from page to page to mark our progress. Also, it helps us to see what's ahead—specifically rest areas and restaurants. For us, the best part of the TripTiks is the diversions they recommend. Along our journey are possible places to stop and linger—and the TripTik provides ideas.

When we create a plan of instruction for our writers, we create an instructional TripTik that takes us from Point A to Point B. We know where we're starting, and we know where we need to end, but our students take us on diversions that require us to stop and linger. In a genre study, a typical instructional time line emerges and we can plan how much time we want to spend on each piece, keeping the possibility of detours in mind. Here's how a model time line based on daily writing instruction across an eight-week unit might be fleshed out.

If our genre study is approximately eight weeks long, we have somewhere between thirty-five and forty lessons to plan in consultation with our students' needs. In many classrooms, I typically see these lessons unfold as follows:

- **Introducing the Genre (One or Two Lessons):** The first few mini-lessons focus on introducing students to the genre we're about to study. Students may read books, view video clips, or listen to representative samples of the genre so they get a sense of what the genre is all about. Teachers ask children to bring in examples from home or to find examples in the classroom library of the genre from the piles of books they are currently reading. The genre study begins through student inquiry and exploration.

- **Reading (Three to Five Lessons):** When students read as writers, their immersion in the reading gives them valuable insights that will teach them how to write within the genre. Students chart what they notice about the genre because their observations and insights inform their writing. Students do this studying individually, in small groups, or in a whole-class setting and begin to develop the knowledge needed to write within the genre.

- **Brainstorming (One or Two Lessons):** Writers spend a mini-lesson or two brainstorming possible topics, audiences, and purposes for their writing within the genre. They also brainstorm publication possibilities that are appropriate for the genre. If writers have a rudimentary understanding of *what* the genre is, teachers can guide them to think of ways they might use this type of writing on their own—and students may come up with ideas we haven't yet considered. Choice in topic is crucial in a student-driven writer's workshop. It's important for young writers to write about topics they are drawn to write about. For example, students might read collections of poetry and decide to create a collection of poems about Mom to give her for Mother's Day. Or students may learn that informational how-tos can teach others how to do something, so the class creates a how-to fair in the cafeteria where they teach others in the school how to do something. In essence, writers begin to think about how they might write *something* that is relevant and meaningful for *someone* who matters.

- **Setting Goals (One to Two Lessons):** Students need an opportunity to set goals for themselves (see Chapter 3). Writers revisit past goals they've established to see if they need to bring them forward into a new genre. They also decide on new goals to set for themselves. Teachers ask students to think about where they want to go as writers and what they want to learn. Students come forward in these mini-lessons to share their goals—getting response from peers and providing examples for other writers. We also set instructional goals for ourselves. I once set the following goal for myself as a writing teacher: *I will commit to writing one page in my daybook at least five days a week and see if that makes me a more productive writer.* When we set goals ourselves, and examine them, we can weave much of what we learn as writers into our instruction.

- **Planning (Two or Three Lessons):** I worry about writers being required to plan in one specific way, such as starting with a graphic organizer that everyone must use. Some students thrive when they have a graphic organizer to help them plan. Some feel constricted or rebel, and subvert the process. Throughout a genre study, we should teach students various ways to plan their writing within the genre. When we see students planning in ways we think would benefit other writers, we can bring them forward as co-teachers in our mini-lessons. For example, as you confer, you may see a student use mind mapping as a planning strategy for informational writing—a strategy you have not explicitly taught.

You might consider asking the student to lead the next mini-lesson focused on planning. Writers need exposure to various ways to plan for a piece of writing. And each writer should decide whether or not the suggestions help him or her compose.

- **Drafting (Five to Seven Lessons):** When studying a specific genre, we need to give students opportunities to draft *multiple* pieces within that genre. They may spend an entire workshop drafting on one topic and then abandon it for an entirely different topic the next day. Or, they may spend three or four days drafting on one topic and then switch to a different topic for three or four days. At the halfway point in a genre study, writers should have many choices for which draft they will take to publication. We need to spend several days allowing writers to draft and showing them different routines that writers use to draft. This is a time when we can weave in the procedural lessons that emerged from studying students. For example, to teach a lesson about staying focused on writing during drafting, we may invite a student to come forward in the mini-lesson and explain how she stays focused during drafting by wearing sound-reducing headphones; then we brainstorm as a class other ways to stay focused during writing.

- **Revising (Thirteen to Fifteen Lessons):** At some point, writers must set deadlines for themselves. A midpoint deadline approaches and, through conferring, you notice that the majority of writers are ready to delve into revising their texts. You can say, "It's time to choose a piece to take to publication." Students choose one, and then they spend a couple of weeks engaged in revision. During these lessons, craft and process lessons coalesce. Students show the beginnings and endings of their texts or the texts of mentor authors and explain how they might revise. Writers dissect structures, text features, words, and voice. Teachers and students talk about how they can elaborate on topics, develop characters, and add stanzas to poems to make them resonate. Writers examine voice and how they might clarify theirs through punctuation. They add illustrations. They use the Internet to conduct research. They learn ways to support arguments, include evidence, and state positions. Writers spend a lot of time revising because revision is when the *real* writing happens.

- **Monitoring Goals (One Lesson):** It's important to instill in our young writers that as they're trudging ahead in their writing, they need to take a moment to breathe and reflect on their progress. Writers might choose a day when they're in the thick of revision to revisit their goals and ask themselves, *How's it going?* Then they continue forward or adjust based on their reflections about their work.

- **Editing (One to Three Lessons):** When writers get closer to publication, they begin the word-by-word, sentence-by-sentence, paragraph-by-paragraph work of editing their writing. Students can do this individually, with a writing partner, or in a writing group. Writers edit their *own* writing because we know this work is best done not through worksheets but in the context of our own writing (Anderson 2005, 2007). Mini-lessons we teach during the editing phase involve new skills that writers add to an evolving editing checklist they carry forward into subsequent genre studies.

- **Publishing (One to Three Lessons):** Depending on our type of publication, children devote little or lots of time to publishing their work. If they're rewriting their piece in their best handwriting, this work may take only a day or so. If they're creating a digital story, we may devote double or triple that amount of time. Writers can take us on diversions by thinking of new, creative ways to publish work that will engage their readers. But we have to make sure this remains manageable for us as teachers. We may give students a couple of different choices for publication—choices that we know will be manageable when we assist in the publication process.

- **Celebrating (One to Two Lessons):** Our deadline has arrived, and it's time for our writing to go public. For each genre study, we *must* take a day of our workshop to celebrate our students' work by allowing time for authentic audiences to read and respond to it. A publication celebration should be an event. And it should stir excitement for our writers. On this day, writers get response from audiences. It may be in the form of a sticky note, a lengthier letter, or a verbal response. Authors set the response agenda by suggesting ways for the audience to respond. Then, each author takes the responses and reflects.

- **Reflecting on Goals (One to Two Lessons):** Finally, writers think closely about their goals. They read and contemplate the response of audiences. They revisit goals sheets and reflect on their progress. They add new artifacts to their writing portfolios to show what they know now that they didn't know before. They engage in a Socratic seminar and discuss, with fellow writers, how they have been transformed as writers. They end one writing chapter and turn the page in anticipation of the next chapter—a new genre study that presents new possibilities.

Digital Diversion: LiveBinders

I maintain several traditional, old-school, three-ring white binders for various genres I teach. My binders are divided into the following sections:

- Mini-Lessons: all my written lesson plans from previous years
- Teacher-Created Products: pieces of writing I created on my own to use in the classroom as demonstration models
- Student-Created Products: photocopies of student work I think would make effective models for future students
- Published Examples: a collection of published texts by authors I use as mentor authors to teach the genre
- Book Lists: lists of books I want to use when students immerse themselves in the genre
- Mini-Lesson Daybook Sheets: half sheets of paper that contain the main focus of mini-lessons I teach; students glue these into their daybooks so they have a record of all our lessons available to them as they write
- Assessment Guides: rubrics or guides the students and I create to use when charting our progress

As you can imagine, this requires a lot of paper! And hard copies are not as easy to update as electronic copies. Good news: we can now create digital binders of our work using LiveBinders (www.livebinders.com), a website that allows you to create your own resources as well as collect various resources from the Internet and organize them into separate folders and subfolders. It also allows you to easily share these binders with colleagues.

My LiveBinder Homepage

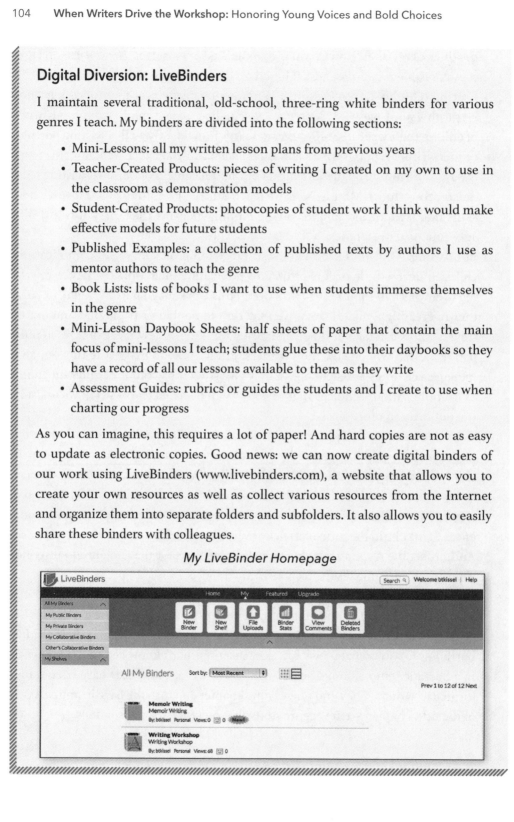

A LiveBinder allows you to create multiple tabs for various categories. You can then add subtabs for each category that will direct viewers to various sites. These are the categories I typically create for my LiveBinders:

- Overview Tab: What is [name of genre]?
- Mini-Lesson Ideas
- Types of Subgenres Within the Genre
- Student-Created Examples
- Lists of Representational Texts
- Teaching Videos (downloaded from YouTube or TeacherTube)

An Example of a Memoir Study

Reflect

At the end of each genre study, as students reflect on their learning, we need to reflect on our instruction. I usually open my daybook and write some thoughts using these questions as guides (see Figure 4.10):

- *What worked?*
- *What didn't work?*
- *What do I need to bring forward to the next genre study?*

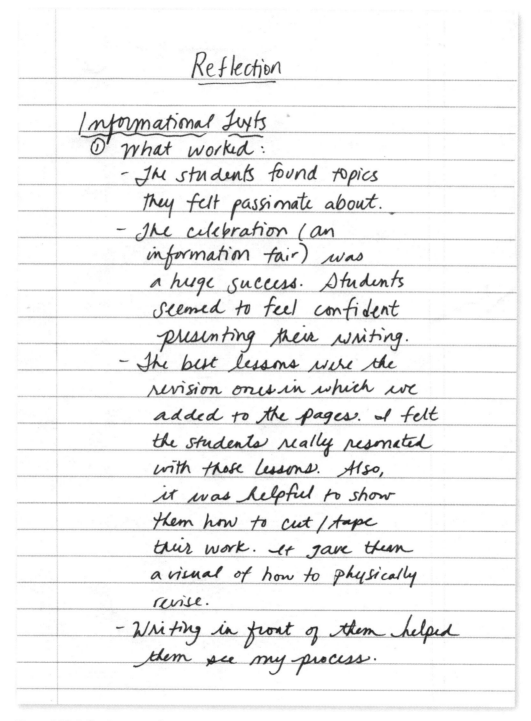

Reflection

Informational Texts

① What worked:
- The students found topics they felt passimate about.
- The celebration (an information fair) was a huge success. Students seemed to feel confident presenting their writing.
- The best lessons were the revision ones in which we added to the pages. I felt the students really resonated with those lessons. Also, it was helpful to show them how to cut/tape their work. It gave them a visual of how to physically revise.
- Writing in front of them helped them see my process.

Figure 4.10 Reflecting on teaching

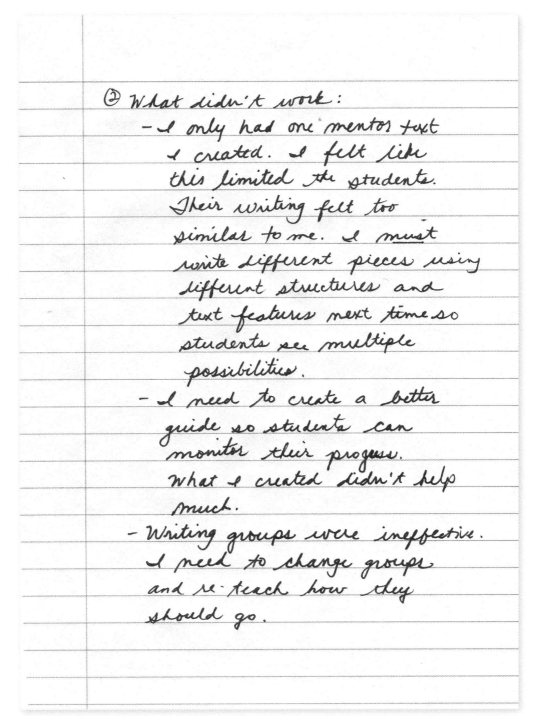

② What didn't work:
- I only had one mentor text I created. I felt like this limited the students. Their writing felt too similar to me. I must write different pieces using different structures and text features next time so students see multiple possibilities.
- I need to create a better guide so students can monitor their progress. What I created didn't help much.
- Writing groups were ineffective. I need to change groups and re-teach how they should go.

Figure 4.10 (continued) Reflecting on teaching

These notes make me aware of how I might revise this study in the future and of the lessons I need to carry forward with me into the next genre study. I learn what worked (such as students finding topics or successful revision lessons) and what didn't work (for example, I may find I need more teacher-created mentor texts or better groupings for writing groups). Then, through careful, thoughtful reflection, I end the genre study and start anew. And the cycle keeps spinning.

Frequently Asked Questions About Mini-Lessons

1. My school purchased a packaged writing curriculum, and I'm required to use it. What should I do?

Use it. But only as a resource. Most packaged curricula I've seen have some effective lessons that specifically address components of a genre. Pull those lessons from the program and weave them into your plans. But if the packaged program gives you a day-to-day sequence of lessons to follow—subvert! If we take notes during conferring and pay attention to what our writers are doing, they will guide the sequence of lessons.

2. I'm told there is a set way of conducting a mini-lesson. It has to be a certain length, and I have to use the same language every time I teach it. Do you agree?

I believe in the ritual of workshop (a mini-lesson, time to write/confer, author's chair, reflection), and I believe routine helps writers (and teachers) maintain focus. I do believe a mini-lesson should be short—the longer the lesson, the more attention we lose. I believe our best lessons are our most direct, focused ones. And those shouldn't take any longer than ten minutes. I also believe mini-lessons should be short because my *real* instruction happens during conferring, and I want to safeguard that time. But I resist using the same language each time I teach a mini-lesson. I think authenticity is my greatest strength as a teacher, so using the same language during every mini-lesson feels too prescribed and robotic to me.

3. How should I bring student writing forward into my mini-lessons?

I bring in students as co-teachers when I see them demonstrate a skill their peers could use in their writing. I talk to writers beforehand and get permission to use their work during a mini-lesson. Then, I have them stand next to me and co-teach alongside me. I use their writing *only* to show effective writing moves. I would never use a writer's work to show what *not* to do, because that would humiliate the writer and create mistrust in the classroom.

4. At our school, one teacher on our team plans writing instruction. It saves us time because each of us takes a subject area and plans for the entire grade level. Why is that a problem?

In a student-driven writing workshop, it's imperative that mini-lessons be developed from a study of our students as writers. The most knowledgeable person to plan those lessons is the person who meets with the writers every day during conferring. A better use of team planning time would be for your teammates to gather and study your conferring notes. Find patterns among all your writers. Then, together, talk about effective lessons that would help all those students, and write those lessons *together*. For mini-lessons focused on genre, study the genre together as a team. Get insight into the genre by being readers and writers yourselves. Conduct a genre study as a team the same way you might conduct a genre study with your students. That will help you spend your time planning for writing instruction more effectively.

5. My school allows only thirty minutes a day to teach writing. How do I teach a workshop in that short amount of time?

First, advocate for more time. If we want writers to get better at writing, they need time to write! However, if that is not possible, preserve as much time for conferring as possible. That means shortening the mini-lesson even further. In a thirty-minute block of time, I usually suggest spending five minutes on a mini-lesson, twenty to twenty-four minutes conferring, and one to two minutes on reflection right after the lesson. Then I suggest doing an author's chair during a transitional time during the day—maybe first thing in the morning, before or after recess or lunch, or at the end of the day. Ideally, you should have a solid forty-five minutes to an hour teaching all the components at once to maintain focus and consistency. But preserve the writing time—even at the expense of a shorter mini-lesson. In my opinion, conferring is a more important use of instructional time.

Travelogue

I recently taught a seminar focused on writing instruction for elementary school teachers. I believe teachers best learn how to teach writing by writing themselves. So, for five days we wrote, talked about what we wrote, discussed how we had taught writing the previous year, and discovered ways to be better writing teachers for our students.

I begin every class I teach with a writing experience—even before we meet one another, we write our way into the day. For this seminar I began by asking teachers to brainstorm a list of places that have been significant in their lives—in good ways or bad. Teachers began listing: childhood homes, a grandparent's house, a country of origin, a school, a backyard, a neighbor's house, a courthouse. They chose one place as a focus for a draft. One teacher chose an orphanage where she found her children. Another chose a prison where she visited her father as a child. Once they chose their topics, the teachers drew. They drew the physical place. Then they drew people within that place.

After a few minutes, I asked teachers to start using words to describe the place and emotions to explain why the place was meaningful to them. They spent about thirty minutes doing so while I walked around and conferred. After thirty minutes, I asked teachers to stop writing and start sharing. They found a partner and read their writing. One brave teacher shared her writing with the whole group—not even knowing the names of the audience yet. She set the response agenda and shared, and the group responded. Tears streamed down the author's face, which is what typically happens when I do writing experiences like this one, and others in the group cried as well.

After a quick reflection, we gathered back together. I asked, "So, what did you think about the workshop?"

A participant responded, "That felt so authentic, so organic. It felt like we were really writing about stuff that mattered to us. Oh, I loved it. I just wish I could teach this way."

"Why can't you?" I asked.

"We use a program the district bought. My literacy coach made some scripted lessons from the program, and we just follow those. We kind of have to follow those lessons."

"Why?" I asked.

She shrugged. "Because if we don't, we get in trouble from admin."

I ended our first writing experience with this statement: "Well, this week we will write. You will come up with your own writing ideas, your own purpose for writing, and your own intended audience. And you will learn a lot about writing by being writers yourselves. I'll adjust writing lessons based on what I see you all doing as writers. I'll ask some of you to share the moves you make as writers with the entire group because others will learn from you. We'll talk a lot about our writing. We'll get in groups and give suggestions to one another. By the end of the week, you'll have something written that you'll be proud to share with your intended audience. I won't use scripts. You'll guide me. And, ideally—*ideally*—you'll gain the agency you'll need to persuade your administrators to think otherwise about scripted writing instruction."

In a negotiated writer's workshop, we create the highway system for travel, and our writers provide the exits and rest stops. We, the more experienced writers, see a potential instructional route to teach a genre. And we speed ahead, going slightly above the speed limit to get writers to their final destination. But along our instructional journey, writers, in the midst of writing, make us slow down. They bring forward new possibilities that cause us to pause. We also experience fender benders along the way—some caused by writers, many of them caused by us, their teachers. When accidents happen, we come to a stop, revise our instruction, and alter our deadlines. And then, wonderfully, there are unexpected diversions. Students take us to exits that promise something different—something that adds flavor to our travel. And we go, because sometimes these excursions end up being the best part of the trip.

Chapter 5

Conditions: Teachers Create Smooth Writing Experiences

*L*ike many of today's teachers, I never took a course in my teacher preparation program that focused solely on teaching writing. I had a course about teaching science, another one focused on social studies, two classes in teaching reading, and another two in teaching math. I took courses in teaching P.E., music, and art. And I had one course in children's literature. But I never took a course focused on teaching writing. So as I started my career, I had no idea what I needed to put in place to help writers flourish in my classroom.

As mentioned in Chapter 1, I found Donald Graves's book *A Fresh Look at Writing* (1994) toward the end of my first year of teaching. One chapter in particular transformed my thinking and instruction. Graves described the conditions that encourage good writing from students:

- *Time* and the importance of prioritizing it so students have daily opportunities to write
- *Choice* and the power that comes from students choosing their own topics for writing
- *Response* and how writers need thoughtful response from readers to change their writing, confirm their decisions, and connect with their work
- *Demonstration* and the teacher's role in providing models for writers to transfer to their own writing
- *Expectation* and the influence of setting high expectations to push the writer forward

- *Room Structure* and creating spaces where writers can roam and find peers to support their work
- *Evaluation* and making sure writers are involved in the process of finding value in their learning

I've witnessed how K–5 teachers have created these conditions in their classrooms. In this chapter, I revisit these conditions and contextualize them by describing what I've seen in classrooms where students drive the workshop. As you read about these classrooms, consider how you might incorporate these conditions into your own rooms. After the description of each one, pause and ponder: *In what ways can I foster conditions so my classroom is more writer driven than teacher driven?*

Time

> *When a teacher asks me, "I can only teach writing one day a week. What kind of program should I have?" my response is, "Don't teach it at all. You will encourage poor habits in your students and they will only learn to dislike writing. Think of something you enjoy doing well; chances are you involve yourself in it far more than one or two times a week."* (Graves 1994, 104)

Over the last decade I have witnessed a transition in literacy instruction. As school districts began reforming the ways they tested writing (less testing) and reading (more testing), instructional time shifted in response. Research on how testing has affected time spent on writing instruction supports what I've witnessed (McCarthey 2008). Two-hour literacy blocks have changed: instead of one hour for reading and one hour for writing, the time spent on writing decreased as time spent on reading increased. As if reading and writing were independent of each other. As if one doesn't reinforce the other.

Graves wrote his book more than twenty years ago, yet teachers still approach me at conferences and workshops and say, "All this stuff you're saying about writing is great and all, but we simply don't have time to teach it." My responses to this comment vary depending upon my level of frustration that day, but typically I respond with my own pointed questions:

- "We would never say we don't have time to teach reading. Why is it okay for us to say we don't have time to teach writing?"
- "Who dictates how you spend your time in your classroom? If it's you, change your schedule. If it's your administrator, have a conversation. Writing instruction should be nonnegotiable."

The answer is simple: If we want students to get better as writers, they need to write.

In order to write, they need time to practice their craft. They need to get into a writing routine in which they engage in writing four to five times a week for thirty minutes to an hour. The more time, the better. We become better runners by running, better swimmers by swimming, better dancers by dancing, better readers by reading, *better writers by writing.*

If you are in charge of your daily instructional schedule, make this time available. If others are in charge of your schedule and writing is not listed as a priority, engage in some conversations with your leadership. Advocate for writing as an essential part of your literacy block. Talk about how writing gives students voice. Explain how writing supports reading; when students study mentor authors, they gain insights into the reading process. Show administrators that when students engage in writing, they are crafting texts full of inference, character development, theme, informational text features, and other aspects that make them stronger readers and thinkers. And if administrators still discourage writing instruction after all your passionate pleading, *subvert!* Smile, appear agreeable, then close your door and teach writing anyway. I live by the motto *Stand up for your beliefs—even if you're standing alone.*

I spent time in one particular teacher's kindergarten classroom recently. She was the only one on her grade level to enact a writer's workshop with her students. She taught writing every day. At the beginning of the year, her workshop lasted thirty minutes. A couple of months into the school year, students had built writing stamina and started demanding more time to keep writing. Their teacher found the time— and something magical happened: Her students wrote and wrote and wrote. They wrote in ways she didn't expect. Authors emerged who had these incredible, powerful stories to share. Then, she started to post their work outside her classroom on the walls of the halls. Other teachers would stop and read the students' work on the way to their classrooms. One day, a fellow kindergarten teacher asked, "How in the world did you get your students to write like this?" She responded, "I just gave them time to write." This is how a writing revolution takes root.

Structured Time

Once teachers are convinced that they *must* teach writing, the follow-up question is, "How do I structure my time?" Ideally, you have a block of uninterrupted time (forty-five to sixty minutes for grades 1–5; thirty to forty-five minutes for kindergarten) to engage in a brief mini-lesson, a chunk of time to confer with students as they write, a small chunk of time to conduct an author's chair, and a couple of minutes to reflect. Look at these components in percentages (Figure 5.1) with the following insights:

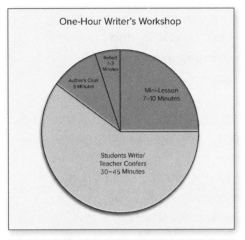

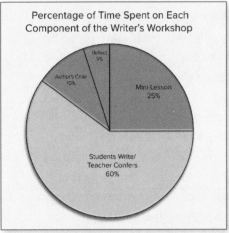

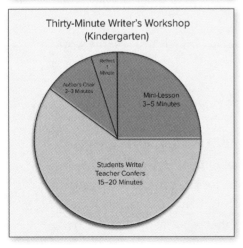

Figure 5.1 Time spent on each component of the writer's workshop

- **Mini-Lessons:** These should be short, direct, and focused. A mini-lesson is information that writers can choose to use that day in their writing, at a later time, or not at all. But if your lesson goes any longer than ten minutes, you'll have young writers rolling around the floor like worms baking in the sun. As you plan, make sure you keep the lesson brief and focused on just one teaching point. Keeping these lessons short allows students more time to write and gives you more time to confer.

- **Conferring/Writing:** This time should be twice as long as all the other elements. Why? Because writers need time to write and teachers need time to meet with individual writers. In less-than-ideal schedules, take time away from the mini-lesson to protect the time you have for conferring and writing. Typically in a sixty-minute writing block, students write for thirty to forty-five minutes while we confer. Younger students need to build stamina before they can write for longer stretches of time.

- **Author's Chair:** Give one or two students the opportunity to share their work at the chair. Younger students with shorter pieces sometimes go faster. Older students with longer, more complex pieces need more time. Remember, students have a short window of attention before their minds wander. Keep this time brief—between five and ten minutes in a sixty-minute block schedule.

- **Reflect:** At the end of the workshop, reserve the last one to two minutes for a quick reflection. Younger students can take a minute to turn, talk, and reflect with a partner. Older students can do a one-to-two-minute quick-write. We can reserve longer stretches of time for deep reflection during specific days of a genre study. As part of the workshop, this is just a small snippet of time.

Writer-Driven Time

There have been times in my life when I have awakened in the morning, sat at a computer, and become so immersed in my writing that I have lost all sense of time. It happened when I wrote my dissertation in graduate school—when I had so many stories to tell about the young writers I had observed that I worried my fingers couldn't type fast enough to record the details. It happened again when writing this book. The noted psychologist Mihaly Csikszentmihalyi (1990) calls this concept *flow*—a highly focused mental state of concentration in which a person is so engaged in an activity, so immersed in the act, that a sense of time vanishes.

Sometimes we can be so driven by a topic, so focused on a purpose and audience for our work, that the act of writing transcends our concept of time. I've seen students from pre-K to college enter this state of *flow* on several occasions. And each time it has happened, it has been because they were driven by a real purpose for their writing, an authentic audience for their work, and a passion for the topic unfolding on the page.

We're bound by time at school. We have other subjects to teach, special classes (e.g., music, P.E., and art) to attend, recess, lunch breaks, and a whole host of other distractions that wreak havoc on our flow. I know many children who, if given the opportunity, could spend two, three, four hours a day writing. And sometimes, *sometimes,* I think we should just allow it.

I spent time as a researcher in a first-grade classroom. One morning when I entered the room, the children were already writing. Their teacher, Mary, greeted me at the door and said, "They begged for a writing day, so I decided to just let them write all morning." And that's what they did. Plans were pushed aside, kids found comfortable spaces, and they spent a glorious morning crafting stories, reading their writing with peers, writing in groups, and being immersed in their six-year-old flow. Writers who drive the workshop also need opportunities to drive the clock sometimes as well.

Choice

When children choose their own topics, I can expect more of their writing. 'What did you set out to do here? Did you have an audience in mind for this?' From the beginning in our conference I can focus my questions on their initiative and their intentions. (Graves 1994, 104)

Before I knew better, I used to assign writing prompts to my second graders. I was under the impression that they didn't have their own stories to tell—or that they were incapable of doing the important thinking work that writers did to choose their own topics. I believed, inaccurately, that my young students were too immature to make decisions for themselves as writers. So even though I did it with the best of intentions, I often took that power away from them. I made their decisions for them.

I remember one day during my first year teaching, I wrote this prompt on the board: "Tell me about a time you went to the beach." I was teaching in downtown Jacksonville, Florida, and the beach was about ten miles from the school. I assumed everyone had been to the beach, and I thought it was a universal topic for everyone in the class. Two children started writing. Twenty-four children sat motionless and stared at me.

"What?" I asked. "What's wrong? Why aren't you writing?"

Trevor looked at me, smirked, glanced at his classmates, and responded, "We ain't never been to no beach!"

This was a transformative check on my white, male, upper-middle-class privilege. First, I had assumed everyone had the same experiences. Second, I had thought everyone shared *my* experiences. Third, and this is difficult to admit, I thought the experiences of those students who didn't share these experiences were somehow deficient. It took me years of teaching, reading, and talking with colleagues who conduct research in culturally responsive teaching to realize how my own biases crept into classroom instruction in pervasive, unconscious ways.

The day I assigned the beach topic was the last day I ever assigned a writing prompt. After reflecting upon that experience, I learned that it wasn't my job to assign *what* writers write; I was tasked with teaching children *how* to write about their topics in fresh, interesting ways. In choosing their topics, students found their passion, and I helped them craft their writing in ways that made their voices resonate.

This is what I learned about students when I stopped prescribing topics and allowed choice:

- Jamela was taken from her mother, adopted by her aunt, and walked to Wendy's after school, where she sat in the dining area and did schoolwork while her aunt worked the cash register.
- Andy loved going to the zoo because he saw animals he had never seen during his early childhood in Cambodia.
- Cynthia was scared of the police because they came to her house once and arrested her mother and the officers kept yelling at her to "shut up and get on the ground!"
- Carter spent a glorious weekend at his family reunion at a park where the food was spread across picnic tables "like a patchwork quilt of deliciousness."

When students choose their own writing topics, we learn about their lives and interests—and sometimes, they tell stories that are difficult for us to hear. Or they write about topics that make us pause. I think often about Ralph Fletcher's book *Boy Writers* (2006) and still see how boy stories and boy interests are marginalized. Any story with a gun or sword (even if the violence is historically based or comic) gets quickly revised, potty humor gets deemed *inappropriate*, and science fiction causes many teachers to roll their eyes.

I also think about the child who writes about her neighborhood and the violence occurring within it, and is asked to tone it down. Or the child who comes to the United States from another country and writes in his home language, only to have his home culture invalidated when he hears he needs to write solely in English. Or the child I wrote about in a recent *Reading Teacher* article who wrote a story about his family using bait dogs for their dog-fighting activities (Kissel and Miller 2015). The boy's teacher didn't censor his story, but many teachers might have. When we tell children, "Don't write about that part of your life," we essentially tell them, "Your experiences don't matter." They do matter. When students choose their topics and we allow them to write about them, we tell students, "Your stories matter."

Writers Choose Their Spaces and Partners.

It's equally important for children to choose their writing spaces. Libby Christian, a second- and third-grade teacher, arranges her classroom in a way that provides multiple spaces for students to write. I spent a morning asking her students why they sat where they sat:

- Brennan (lying on his stomach, on the carpet in the middle of the classroom, papers spread out): "I'm sitting here because I like to spread out. I put all my pages for my book around me so I can see them all. I lie on my stomach because it just feels good to me. And I don't like anyone around me because I just need my space."
- Izzy and Jenny (sitting side by side at a table in the middle of the classroom): *Jenny:* "We like to work together. We give each other really good ideas for our stories. So we sit over here, together, and talk about our stories and just help each other out." *Izzy:* "And I like to help her make her drawings since I'm good at drawing."
- Jill (lying in an enclosed cubby usually reserved for backpacks, feet pushed against one end of the cubby, knees bent, notebook placed in lap): "I love writing in here. It's like my own little room. Ms. Christian made these comfortable pads

to sit on, and I have these pillows for my back. When I sit in here to write, I'm just in my own little world."

- Mark, Peter, Kai, and Asher (four boys sitting together as a cluster at a table): *Peter:* "We always sit together. We like to tell each other our stories while we're writing them." *Asher:* "Sometimes we probably talk too much. But it's kind of nice to have some friends around when I'm writing." *Kai:* "I crack up at Mark's stories. They're hilarious."

A classroom where choice is a fundamental value, where writers choose where to sit and with whom to write, provides more ways to keep students engaged and in control of their decisions.

Writers Choose the Genre.

In this era of Common Core, we've become rather genre focused in our instruction—particularly in the modes of narrative, informational writing, and persuasive writing. And I do advocate for systemic study of multiple genres throughout the school year. When students are able to go deep within genres to understand how authors craft their books using features specific to those genres, they become writing insiders. It's important for students to know how to navigate their writing across multiple genres, because we write in varied contexts.

Occasionally, however, I've found myself confronted by a writer who asks, "Do I have to write an informational report? I'd rather keep working on the chapter book I started writing." And I'm conflicted. If I say yes, I worry they won't get the experience of writing within a genre that makes them stretch beyond their comfort zone. If I say no, I've eliminated their power to make their own decision and they may disengage as writers.

I've discovered a compromise. At the beginning of a genre study, teachers can require students to publish *one* piece within that genre at the end of the six-to-eight-week study. But that shouldn't be the *only* piece a writer works on for six to eight weeks.

To illustrate: In Diana Hosse's fifth-grade classroom, one boy wanted to write exclusively about basketball. Being a brilliant writing teacher, Diana encouraged his passion by having him write about basketball in a variety of genres (for example, a biography of Michael Jordan, a collection of basketball poems, a memoir about winning a basketball game). She compromised when her genre focus was poetry and the boy wanted to write an informational text instead. They conferred:

Student: Can't I just write about the rules of basketball today instead of poems?

Diana: Sure. It's your choice. But on February 15, we're heading down to the coffee shop to share our poems at open-mic day. You will need to read from your collection of poems. That means you'll need some poems to read. Have you written any yet?

Student: I have a couple so far. I just don't feel like writing another poem today.

Diana: It's totally fine with me if you want to write something else today as a writer. But keep in mind our deadline. You'll need a collection of poems by February 15. It'll be up to you to manage your writing time in here to make sure that gets done.

As writers, many of us are often working on multiple pieces at one time. Just yesterday I wrote the following: a get-well letter to a colleague who is sick, e-mails to my students reminding them of what to bring to class next week, notes based on a Socratic seminar conducted in my graduate class last night, a note to my son's teacher about homework, a text to my wife to remind her to get the kids, a short list of groceries, feedback about a job candidate visiting our campus, and a lesson plan for Friday's class. Multiple genres, multiple purposes, multiple modes, multiple audiences, *one* day of writing. If we, as adults, work on multiple pieces at one time, within multiple genres, why shouldn't our students?

If we value choice, then genre should be another choice available to our writers. We encourage our students to play around in new, unfamiliar genres and teach them the possibilities contained within them. We even help them set purposes, audiences, and deadlines to write pieces within the genre. But at the same time, we don't eliminate genres from our writers who write with passion within them. When we compromise, we expand rather than restrict the choices for writers.

Writers Choose Their Audiences and Purposes.

If you ever want to get a sense of whether writers are writing for you or for others, ask them, "Why are you writing this? Who are you writing this for?" If they respond, "I'm writing this for *you* because *you told me to*," then they are just *doing school*. They are not really participating in authentic writing experiences.

Writers who write with passion do so because they have reasons other than to simply please the teacher. When Diana Hosse set out to teach persuasive writing with her fifth graders, she began by posing the following questions: "What do you want to change in the world? How can you make a difference?"

Students offered all sorts of responses, from helping animals to ending war. But the student who was most passionate was Alana, a young immigrant from a village in Kenya.

Alana: I want to do a clothing drive for my village. Where I come from, people always need clothes. And we have so many clothes here. So I thought we could collect clothes here and send them over there.

Diana: Yes! Great idea! How are you going to use writing to persuade people to donate clothes?

Alana and three of her peers pondered this question for weeks and developed a plan to advocate for their cause. They composed an e-mail to get large boxes donated. Then, they situated the boxes throughout the school with large signs asking people to donate clothes. They wrote a commercial, filmed themselves, and played it for the school to build awareness about their project. And they were convincing! By the end of their eight-week genre study, Alana and her friends had collected ten large boxes of clothing. They learned about the generosity of their school community. More important, they learned how powerful writing can be when we use it to reach *real* audiences for *real* purposes.

I have visited many classrooms in which young writers write for authentic audiences and purposes:

- A kindergarten class contacted a local food bank. The children crafted interview questions with the teacher about the food bank's needs. Then they Skyped with the food bank director and asked their questions. When the children found out the food bank needed canned goods and diapers, the kindergartners drew pictures (and, if they were able, wrote words to accompany their drawings) of the needed supplies. They took their drawings and writings home and collected the needed items from their families and neighbors.

- In a first-grade classroom, children combined art and writing. As the children studied multiple artists, they created artwork in similar styles and wrote text about their artistic process to accompany each piece. They posted the artwork on walls throughout the classroom and the outside hall and then invited parents to attend a gallery crawl. When parents came to visit, the children took them around the room and described their artwork and how they created it.

- I observed a second-grade classroom of students who studied biographies of famous Americans in an interesting, interactive way; students eventually chose one person they admired and wrote a biography. Then, taking the information they learned through their study, they wrote speeches. They dressed as their person and performed their speeches for others in the school, helping others learn about their person as well.

- Children in a third-grade classroom created multigenre projects about an important event or person in their lives. Combining poetry, memoir, informational text, and persuasive essays, students created a published book that could be read by peers, family members, and any other audience member who wanted to know more about the child's life.
- Fourth graders wrote collections of poems. At the end of their poetry study, they dressed in all-black outfits, wore berets, and read their poems at a local coffeehouse. Whoever happened to be in the coffeehouse at the time heard writers read their poems aloud. The audience members snapped their fingers at the end of each performance.
- A fifth-grade class, in consultation with their art and music teachers, wrote an opera based on a retelling of *Pink and Say* by Patricia Polacco. The students wrote an adapted script, wrote music and lyrics for several songs in music class, and created the sets in art class. Then they performed their opera for every class in the school.

Students are most passionate about writing when their published pieces go somewhere else besides a folder marked Completed Work. For writers to stay engaged in writing, they need to publish—and they need audiences besides the teacher to respond authentically to their work. When they are empowered to choose those audiences and purposes, they have meaningful reasons to write.

Response

Students need to hear the responses of others to do their writing, to discover what they do or do not understand. The need to help students know how to read their own work, and the work of their classmates, provides further teaching and demonstration opportunities. (Graves 1994, 108)

In her book *When Writers Read* ([1985] 2005), Jane Hansen talks about the important response conditions writers need to thrive: they need teachers and fellow writers to be both response-ible and response-able with their response. This is what those terms mean to me:

- **Response-ible:** Respectfully providing feedback to the writer in a way that supports rather than defeats. Writers should receive constructive feedback, but it has to be done in a way that encourages the writer to keep going—keep improving.

- **Response-able:** Capable of providing feedback because you, a fellow writer, know something about writing. Writers who are *able* to respond have this ability because they've been there before as a writer.

For teachers, response typically happens when conferring with writers. For students, however, response happens when they are engaged with a partner or in small writing groups. Because writers receive so much response from peers, teachers need to help set the response conditions so writers respond response-ibly and response-ably to one another. Mini-lessons help facilitate this talk (see Figure 5.2).

Responsible Talk

Encourage

- This is where I think your writing was very strong:
- This is a memorable section to me:
- Your strengths as a writer are . . .
- This is how I think your audience is going to respond to this:

Suggest

- As a reader, I got a little confused here:
- What if you tried this instead:
- Can I make a suggestion for you?
- This section was a little unclear to me. Could you tell me more?

Question

- What's the one thing you're trying to say in your writing? Did you say it?
- What are you going to do next in your writing?
- What parts of your piece are you not sure about?
- How do you think your audience is going to respond to this?

Figure 5.2 Mini-lesson sheet for responsible talk

Responders face a delicate balance when offering response to writers. The young writer's ego is fragile, and the response has to come forward in a way that doesn't sound too judgmental, too prescribed, or too condescending. I would say this is different for adult writers, but I'd be lying. I've experienced such cutting response from others that I know how it feels for writers to have their confidence rattled. Writing puts our hearts out there and makes us vulnerable, no matter how mature or skilled we are—but especially when we're young and inexperienced. We have to be especially careful when responding to young writers, new to writing, who are forming their literacy identity.

During my research in K–5 classrooms, I interview young writers to gauge how they perceive themselves as writers. Their responses are illuminating, particularly because I believe students' perceptions of themselves as writers have been influenced by the various ways others have responded to their writing. I asked children to describe themselves as writers, specifically whether they saw themselves as strong writers or weak writers. The following is just a sampling of their responses:

- **Ken (kindergarten):** "I'm a good writer. People laugh when I read my stories."
- **Naomi (first grade):** "I'm the worst writer in my classroom. I'm a terrible writer. My letters go all over the place. Sometimes the other kids make fun of my writing because it doesn't look right."
- **Sara (second grade):** "I think I'm a so-so writer. I think there's ways I could be better. My teacher always gives me different ways I could do something better."
- **Tom (third grade):** "I'm a pretty decent writer. I can always come up with some good ideas to write about, and my friends will come to me and ask me to help them come up with some ideas for their writing, too."
- **Luke (fourth grade):** "Well, I used to think I was a pretty good writer, but then I read some of Helen's writing. Have you read it? Whoa! It's *really* good. Kind of blows my writing out of the water. I don't think I'll ever be as a good as her."
- **Elizabeth (fifth grade):** "When we did our gallery walk, and others read my writing, I got a lot of compliments about it. I think poetry is my thing. I think I'm good at it. At least my friends think I'm pretty good at it."

This is just a sampling, but there are patterns across the grade levels. When children describe themselves as writers, their perceptions are often formed by the response of others. Ken and Elizabeth formed their writing identities based on peers' feedback about their strengths (humor, poetry); Sara sees herself as a fair writer because her teacher suggests revisions. Tom feels confident because other children ask him for suggestions. Each perception of self was formed from someone else's response. Responses like these make a strong case for teaching young children how to respond to each other in response-ible and response-able ways.

Writers Work in Writing Groups.

Bringing children together in writing groups can be a powerful way to build their capacity for responding to one another. Writing groups offer an important space for writers to get response from peers. For our youngest children, who are moving away from egocentricism and toward awareness of others, writing groups may be their first foray into listening about others' lives and responding to them. For many K–1 writers, the author's chair provides a good model for how they might respond to one another in quick, focused writing groups. For older writers, however, writing groups provide a special, influential space. For many writers, peers can suggest rich, detailed feedback about a topic that a teacher may not be able to provide.

I conducted research in one fourth-grade classroom in which I asked writers, "What makes a bigger difference to you as a writer: conferring with your teacher or meeting with your small writing group?" I expected children to say that their individual conferences with the teacher were more influential; they didn't—especially the boys.

The following conversation unfolded when I met with one group of boy writers:

Brian: You three have been working in a group together for a while now. Tell me, what's the difference between conferring with your teacher and meeting as a writing group?

Mark: I mean, my teacher gives fine feedback, but she has no idea how to skateboard. And I'm writing about skateboarding. So, she can't offer me any suggestions about how to write about skateboarding. But my friends can. They know what I'm talking about.

Sam: I love my teacher, don't get me wrong. But sometimes I read my writing to her and she doesn't get it. Like, she doesn't laugh at the parts that I want readers to laugh at. Whenever I read my story to friends, they always laugh at the right parts.

Tom: Most of the time the teachers don't get our writing. It's just not their thing, you know. I have all this stuff about this spaceship I'm writing about—like what each of the buttons do when you push them and about how my characters can get from one place to another as holograms—and I'm reading all this stuff to her and she is completely lost. I mean, I write a lot of details, but I kind of feel like she wants me to speed it up or something. Like she wants me to talk about how the characters feel. But I think it's more interesting to talk about the spaceship.

Mark: She's a really great teacher, though. Really. She is. Like, she did help me figure out a really great beginning for my writing. And she taught me how to put it all together so it makes sense.

Tom: Yes. She is a great teacher. She gets us thinking. And she gives us time to write. I just think the writing group helps me more. I think they get my writing a little bit more. That's all.

As teachers, we sometimes believe our response is the most important for our writers. But if we've truly created a classroom environment in which our writers write for their own purposes and audiences, then it's healthy for our students to see their peers as the more influential responders. And, I would argue, it's a sign that the classroom is much more writer driven than teacher driven. The teacher mentioned in the dialogue above was, in fact, a great writing teacher—as her students insisted—because she not only established a classroom in which students were response-ible and response-able, but she also recognized the power of peer feedback and choice of writing partners. She knew how to guide students through mini-lessons and conferences but allowed her students to teach one another about how to make writing decisions for an audience. That's huge.

Demonstration

You, the teacher, are the most important factor in creating a learning environment in your classroom. (Graves 1994, 109)

We teachers provide the best demonstration for writing by being writers ourselves. When we carry daybooks, write frequently, reflect on our writing, and write for authentic audiences, we become the insiders our students need us to be. I would lose credibility and authenticity if I talked to students about what it means to be a writer yet never picked up a pencil and wrote myself. The most powerful way for us to demonstrate is to build a writing life for ourselves.

Teachers Demonstrate Writing Habits.

When we take the challenge to craft a writing life for ourselves, we begin to develop writing habits. These are my habits:

- **I maintain a daybook:** Each semester I purchase a composition book that serves as my daybook. I carry it with me whenever I go someplace. I'm never without it—and it's there for me, like a friend, ready for me to write in it whenever I need to jot something down.

- **I find a comfortable writing spot:** I have two places where I write. I write either on my cherry-red couch in the living room or, if I'm feeling professional, in my upstairs office where I sit on a leather office chair that I spin in when I need to think.
- **I drink caffeine:** I cannot write without caffeine. In the morning, a steaming cup of coffee rests on the right side of my computer. In the afternoon, it's unsweetened iced tea—one lemon, one packet of *Sweet'N Low*. I shouldn't admit I need caffeine to write, but I do.
- **I find a good time to write:** I write more coherently in the morning, but I tend to be more reflective when I write in the evening. In the morning, I wake with new thoughts. In the evening, after I've lived with those thoughts for a while, I often revise my thinking. My daytime is consumed with teaching, feeding children, and housework. The hours from 8:30 a.m. to 7:00 p.m. are shot. So I typically write early (6:30 to 8:30 a.m.), later (7:00 to 10:00 p.m.), or when I have a few quick, quiet moments during the day.
- **I live life so I have something to write about:** Writers need to live so they have something to write about. Throughout the week, and especially on weekends, our family goes on hikes, visits museums, plays sports, and does all the leisurely things that make life fun. We try to live in the moment and live lives worth writing about. Occasionally, when we have a quiet moment together in the house, my family members see me open my daybook and jot something down. Just as it's important for them to see me read, it's important for them to see me write.

What are your writing habits? Many teachers tell me that they don't see themselves as writers. This is a familiar story that has been retold in the research about teachers as writers over the past several decades (Bridge and Heibert 1985; Faery 1993; Hollingsworth 1988; Draper, Barksdale-Ladd, and Radencich 2000). They say, "I ask my children to write biographies, but I don't think I've ever written one."

If you don't have any writing habits, don't beat yourself up. Begin with a notebook, find a comfortable spot, and create some time (even if it's just ten minutes) to sit and write. Do it daily. Make it feel like a natural part of your everyday life. And notice what transpires on the page. Anne Lamott, one of my favorite writers, hilariously writes about ways of finding time to write in her essay "Time Lost and Found" (2010). She says, "First of all, no one needs to watch the news every night, unless one is married to the anchor. Otherwise, you are mostly going to learn more than you need to know about where the local fires are, and how rainy it has been: so rainy! That is half an hour, a few days a week, I tell my students. You could commit to writing one page a night, which, over a year, is most of a book." In essence, we find time for those things we deem worthy of our time.

After you've formed a writing habit, bring those habits into your classroom lessons. Current research shows it takes anywhere from twenty-one to sixty-six days to form a true habit, but I don't think you need to wait that long to talk about your writing habits with your students. Demonstrate that you are a writer, too. It adds to your credibility as a teacher. If we are to teach writing, we must write ourselves and shape our own writing identities. Forming writing habits is the first step (see Figure 5.3).

In *A Writer Teaches Writing* (2004), Donald Murray describes his daybook as a tool that goes with him wherever he goes—a repository of his thinking and creativity. Lil Brannon, Sally Griffin, Karen Haag, Tony Iannone, Cindy Urbanski, and Shana Woodward—a group of professors and teacher-researchers—describe how they use daybooks in their elementary, middle, high school, and college settings (2008). Their students use daybooks to help organize thoughts, build connections between reflection and application, and foster deeper thinking.

Each semester begets a new daybook. I always purchase four or five daybooks during back-to-school sales, when composition books are twenty-five cents each. For one birthday, my wife gave me a composition book cover from an Etsy shop, so I can slide my daybook into the cover whenever I start a new one, and slide it right back out when it's filled. As I began writing this book, I skimmed through past daybooks to discover what they contained. Mostly, they contained the following:

- lesson ideas and lesson plans
- notes from my discussions with students
- bubble maps of ideas for books, journal articles, and book chapters
- drawings—because sometimes what I'm thinking is best conveyed through doodling
- grocery lists—because I can't find any other scraps of paper around the house
- reflections about my teaching
- funny things my children say
- stories from my past to try to make sense of difficult things I experienced in childhood

Figure 5.3 Inside Brian's daybook

- rants about what I hear during meetings (because it's safer than shouting out what I *really* think)
- clippings from magazines and newspapers written by my favorite authors such as Rick Bragg from *Southern Living*, Jon Wertheim from *Sports Illustrated*, David Brooks, Charles Blow, and Gail Collins from the *New York Times*, Kay McSpadden from the *Charlotte Observer*, Ta-Nehisi Coates from the *Atlantic*, and former columnists Anna Quindlen and Dave Barry
- handouts I gather from attending conferences or talks
- church bulletins
- notes I write from attending guest lectures
- lines of dialogue from movies and television shows
- memorable lines from my favorite books

My daybook is a constant companion. It goes wherever I go. And it has, over time, become a reliable friend. When I talk to children about their daybooks, I show them mine. They see my daybook filling up with all sorts of varied, interesting pieces. Over time, their daybooks do the same.

When I first introduced daybooks to students, I controlled the content. Then I realized they had become *my* daybooks, not *theirs*. Restrictive, prescribed daybooks don't work for us as writers—and they don't for our students. Such an epiphany comes from being immersed in writing ourselves. And keeping a daybook can be a valuable tool to help us understand that.

Figure 5.3 (continued) Inside Brian's daybook

Teachers Demonstrate Writing Processes.

Some of the scariest teaching we do is spontaneous writing in front of the class. To demonstrate getting ideas for writing, planning, drafting, revision, and editing, I will often stand in front of the class and provide insight into my process. It's a strange exercise—speaking out loud what's happening inside my head—but I think it's important for young writers to hear our processes expressed.

In a second-grade classroom, where I spent time studying writers, I wrote down the exact words of a teacher beginning a persuasive piece of writing. To begin her piece, she stood in front of the class and talked aloud as she began to generate ideas for writing:

Hmm . . . So we're about to start a genre study on persuasive writing. Okay. Well, if persuasive writing is about coming up with an opinion and I need reasons to support my opinion, I need to think of some ideas.

What's happening in my life right now that might make sense for me to write in this genre? Hmm . . . My children want to play video games during the week. I want them to play only on the weekend, but they are nagging me like crazy about it. I could write my reasons why video games are bad for them and share my reasons with them. Oh . . . My husband wants turkey for Christmas dinner, but I think ham is a better choice—I can do more things with the leftovers. That's a possibility. Here's another one: Mr. [principal] wants to spend our teacher work-day in meetings. But there's so much stuff I need to do in our classroom. I could write him why I think we should have some of that time in our classrooms.

So, which idea is the most important one to me right now? If I'm going to spend a lot of time working on this, what idea matters? I think I want to write the letter to the principal. Maybe it will make some sort of difference.

Analysis of her language reveals important lessons she imparted to her students (see Figure 5.4).

When teachers demonstrate their process, and make their process explicit for student writers, they provide powerful models for children who need guidance as they engage in their own process.

Teachers Demonstrate Authentic Human Emotions.

As writing teachers, we must demonstrate authentic human reactions to a writer's struggles and triumphs. When children struggle to generate ideas for topics, we demonstrate persistence. When children struggle to get their ideas onto the paper, we demonstrate patience. When children struggle to revise their writing because the potential changes feel overwhelming, we demonstrate resilience. When children struggle through the word-by-word, line-by-line tediousness of editing, we demonstrate the importance of working hard. And when our children demonstrate success in any of these areas, we high-five, we clap, and we give reassuring pats on the back.

I once taught a second grader who felt incredibly anxious whenever it was time for writer's workshop. He struggled to come up with ideas. Then, when he had an idea, he struggled to write it on the page. He struggled to spell words, and he knew his writing was often illegible to readers. Some days when I read his writing, the page was damp with tears. I sat next to him and offered reassurance. I told him I would help him find

Well, if persuasive writing is about coming up with an opinion and I need reasons to support my opinion . . .	**Lesson:** What defines "persuasive writing?"
I need to think of some ideas.	**Lesson:** The writer is responsible for coming up with ideas.
Hmm . . . My children want to play video games during the week. I want them to play only on the weekend, but they are nagging me like crazy about it. I could write my reasons why video games are bad for them and share my reasons with them. *Oh . . . My husband wants turkey for Christmas dinner, but I think ham is a better choice—I can do more things with the leftovers. That's a possibility.* *Here's another one. Mr. [principal] wants to spend our teacher workday in meetings. But there's so much stuff I need to do in our classroom. I could write him why I think we should have some of that time in our classrooms.*	**Lesson:** The writer names topic possibilities.
So, which idea is the most important one to me right now?	**Lesson:** The writer chooses the topic that is most important to him or her.
If I'm going to spend a lot of time working on this, what idea matters?	**Lesson:** Writers evaluate their topic possibilities.
I think I want to write the letter to the principal. Maybe it will make some sort of difference.	**Lesson:** Writers make the final decision.

Figure 5.4 Analysis of teacher's language

his way into writing and we would brainstorm ways to get his words out—even if it meant typing them onto a computer. I told him that he would get better and better the more we worked on it together and that I would be by his side the whole year to support him. I could tell he felt better after the conversation, and eventually he put down a couple of words. I celebrated the two words and encouraged him to put down a few more. When he did that, I celebrated some more. He needed a coach and a cheerleader—and I was happy to be both.

Writing can be arduous—and sometimes the only thing that gets the writer through the process is someone else's demonstration of real, authentic, human emotion.

Expectation

I have high expectations for every one of my students. To have high expectations is a sign of caring. (Graves 1994, 110)

I'm on a crusade to eradicate the terms *low* and *high* as adjectives for our students. I hear this terminology all the time in schools or when I engage in professional development. A teacher might say, "This is something I'm doing with my *low* students." Or, "I can do a lot more with my *high* students because they are ready for something new." Here's language that makes me cringe even more: "I have to give my *low* students topics to write about. They just don't have many life experiences." I disagree. All students have experiences. Perhaps we are just uncomfortable with the stories they tell.

The problem with describing our students as *low* and *high* is that they become fixed in those descriptions. The *low* children are considered *low* the entire school year—as if they can never grow, or certainly can't grow as much as other children in the classroom. And, insidiously, this description of the child gets passed on to the next teacher, then the next, and the next. In many schools, students get ability grouped in low, medium, and high classes with homogenous groups of "low," "medium," and "high" peers. It doesn't take long for children to take on that label themselves. Then we wonder why, by middle school, they hate reading and writing and by high school they drop out entirely. We cannot damn an entire generation of writers simply by not expecting much from them.

Peter Johnston (2004, 2012) writes about the power teachers have in the language they use with their students. Similarly, I've witnessed the powerful ways teachers combat the scourge of low expectations through the words they speak to students:

- In a second-grade classroom, I sat near a teacher and listened in on a conference he had with a boy. The boy sat, arms folded, scowl on his face, and a blank page on the table in front of him. Each time the boy said, "I can't," the teacher countered with, "You can." After a two-to-three-minute stalemate, the teacher finally said, "You can. I believe in you. I can help. But you *can* do this!" With patience, and love, the boy scrawled his first sentence and his teacher gave him a fist pump. The conference ended with the teacher saying, "You can. And you did!"

I've also seen how students can use supportive language to support their peers and themselves.

- In a fourth-grade classroom, I listened in as two boys negotiated the authorship of a shared writing. One boy, Hector, said, "You're way better at writing the words, so you write and I'll draw." His partner, Juan, disagreed. "We're both good at writing the words. You write one page, I'll write the next page." Juan refused to allow Hector out of his authorship. Juan had high expectations of his friend.

- Lucas, a fourth grader, reflected on his writing day in a two-minute quick-write. "I didn't think I would be good at writing poems. I surprised myself. I think maybe I am pretty good at this."

Teachers and students can support writers by expecting *writers* to set high expectations for *themselves*. When writers set goals for themselves, we see to it that they work toward those goals—and reach them. When we confer with writers, we tell them what's present on the page and what's not present *yet*, and help them set goals and plan next steps to make their writing even stronger. When we trust students to respond to one another appropriately in groups, we expect for them to talk about writing and hold them accountable if they waste that time instead.

Room Structure

The writing classroom requires a high degree of structure. When children face the empty page, they suddenly feel alone and want to talk or move around the room. (Graves 1994, 111)

A writer needs a physical space that makes writing comfortable and a psychological space that makes being a writer *feel* comfortable. It's similar to the spaces we create at home for our children. When my twin boys were active toddlers, we did a lot to ensure a safe, productive environment for them: we sectioned off rooms with baby gates, put safety plugs into the outlets, and moved anything breakable to a higher place. To keep them engaged as learners, we brought in a bookshelf and bean bags for a reading corner, a play kitchen with props, a box of dress-up clothes, a tool table for their plastic hammers, and exercise balls to bounce around on. Then, as they engaged

Figure 5.5 Libby Christian's classroom writing spaces

in the physical space, we nurtured their psychological spaces: we soothed them when they cried, refereed arguments, cuddled with them as we read books, and laughed when they acted goofy.

It's this basic foundation—safety, love, and belonging as described by Maslow in his hierarchy of needs (Maslow, Frager, and Cox 1970)—that provides our children with the tools to grow as human beings. This is as important for school environments as it is in home environments. Comfortable, safe, and secure physical and psychological spaces help writers thrive.

Physical Spaces

Since 2010, I've followed teachers Mary Mayo (K–1), Libby Christian (grades 2–3), and Diana Hosse (grades 4–5) as they loop with one class of children from one grade level to the next. Although the three teachers have different personalities and teaching styles, their classroom spaces are remarkably similar (see Figure 5.5). Every time I enter their classrooms, I feel like I'm back in my living room at home. Their classrooms are not just learning spaces; they're living spaces.

Gathering Spaces

Each of their classrooms centers on a large carpet—big enough for the entire class to sit together in a common area for the mini-lesson. Framing the carpet are sofas, rocking chairs, and bean bags. Some children sit on the carpet for the mini-lesson. Some sit on the sofa and chairs. Each teacher sets a routine so the chairs are shared equitably among the students.

The teachers situate themselves among their students when it's time to teach. Mary gathers her little ones using musical cues and sits on a rocking chair facing the class. Libby stands among the children, shifting from the front of the carpet to the back

Figure 5.5 (continued) Libby Christian's classroom writing spaces

while moving a document camera that displays models of writing with her. Diana has a long, low table. It houses the mini-lesson glue-ins that children will place in their daybooks and holds her document camera, where she often displays students' work to use during the lesson. The teachers teach among the students in these shared spaces.

The gathering space is the setting for the mini-lesson, the author's chair, and reflection time. Importantly, it's a flexible space. Students can sit in rows to face the teacher for the mini-lesson. Later, they can sit in a circle and face the writer who shares at the author's chair. They can stay in that same circle to have a Socratic discussion to reflect on their learning. Students can shift their bodies to face partners or weave themselves into small groups. The gathering space is like a home's hearth. Everyone gathers to warm up, hear stories, and share the day's events.

Writing Spaces

At the end of mini-lessons, Mary, Libby, and Diana ask students to find *their* spaces for writing. No space in the classroom is off-limits. Some of Mary's kindergartners take battery-powered lanterns and write under tables. Some of Libby's third graders sit in cubbies converted into tight reading/writing nooks. Some of Diana's fifth graders float over to computers to compose or round tables to write with a group. In all three classrooms, there are multiple places where young children can write.

Within their writing spaces, writers contort their bodies in any configuration that keeps them focused. Mary might have some little ones sitting on exercise balls, bouncing up and down as they compose. Libby's students might be lying on their stomachs or on their backs, writing on clipboards with pages of their stories spread out across the space. Diana's students might bring their writing over to a table under a window, needing natural light to inspire some good revision. Never do these three teachers tell children *where* they must write. Writers decide. And, they tend to make choices that work for them. Those who yearn for quiet, stillness, and solitude find a place in the room that provides it. Those who gain energy from working collaboratively find shared spaces to share ideas. When writers determine their writing spaces, they find spaces that meet their needs.

Conferring Spaces

Mary, Libby, and Diana don't ask children to come to them to confer. They go to their students. They meet students in the spaces where writers are working. They find a writer and sit side by side to confer. This says something about the power dynamic in their classrooms, doesn't it? In Mary, Libby, and Diana's classrooms, the teachers view themselves as co-writers. They don't hover over their students, invading their spaces. They engage in conversations. And real conversations don't happen with one person sitting and the other standing above him or her; conversations happen when two people see each other face-to-face.

Psychological Spaces

Writing is a scary endeavor, and sharing our writing with others makes us vulnerable to judgment. Inevitably, writers who share their writing with peers often begin their reading by apologizing: "This is just a draft. It's not really my best work yet." Or, "I'm not really a good writer, but I'll just read it and you can tell me what you think." Writers set low expectations for the responders—bracing for negative feedback and preparing for the hit to their self-esteem. In classrooms where teachers and peers build safe psychological spaces, writers read their work without reservation.

In Lisa Humphries's kindergarten classroom, the kids gathered for an author's chair. It was the beginning of the school year, and students were still learning writing routines. One girl shared her writing with the class and another little boy laughed at her writing—hurting her feelings. Lisa asked the little boy to meet her away from the class toward the back of the classroom, where she offered him a stern but loving rebuke to his response: "You need to know that it's never okay to laugh at someone's hard work. Your friend was sharing her writing with everyone. It's important for us to support her. We want her to keep sharing her work, so we never make fun. Okay?" The young boy understood. He never laughed at the author in the author's chair again.

Lisa, Mary, Libby, and Diana all teach at the same school where each school day begins with the Pledge of Allegiance, followed by a schoolwide statement—the "I Am" creed written by motivational speaker Mark Scharenbroich:

"I Am" Creed

I am unique in the world,

I am capable of learning and growing,

I am a person who appreciates the differences in others,

I am talented and I share my talents,

I am unlike any other human being;

I am a person who pursues personal dreams,

I am an active participant in life,

I am committed to my values;

I am a one-of-a-kind human being and a celebration of life.

Recitation of the creed is followed by a standing ovation, a practice in which one chosen student sits in a chair while the rest of the class members tell the student the ways in which he or she matters. The class sits in a circle on the rug, and the recipient of the standing ovation hears a litany of compliments. The student learns that his or her friends and teachers care, recognize the good choices the student makes, and value the student's friendship, effort, and grace with which the student lives his or her life.

Both the "I Am" creed and the standing ovation happen before writing begins, but the effects of both spill over into the workshop. When writers feel secure in safe psychological spaces, knowing they are learning in classrooms where their friends care about them, they can take risks as writers without fearing their risks will be mocked. Others may disregard these practices as too touchy-feely—as time that could be better spent on academic work. I might have believed that myself before I knew better. But after spending years in these classrooms, I've seen the cumulative effect of these practices on the way young children see themselves as human beings. In a student-driven workshop, students who feel the security and support of classmates also feel less vulnerable when they share their writing with others.

Evaluation

When children choose their own topics, they need to know how to decide if their choices are good ones. They need to know how to evaluate their own work. (Graves 1994, 112)

If we empower students to set high expectations for themselves, we must expect them to evaluate themselves carefully as well. Too often, school districts and teachers take it upon themselves to evaluate student work—leaving the one who crafted the work out of the process. When writers evaluate, they look inward to discover what they know and what they don't know, what they've accomplished and what they haven't accomplished yet, and what they want from their teachers and what they no longer need. When writers evaluate, they discover what's valuable about their learning (Hansen [1985] 2005). This important type of evaluation comes as students reflect on their work and is an extension of what happens during the reflection portion of the workshop. In a writer-driven workshop, evaluation doesn't come from the teacher; it comes from the writer.

Writers Value Their Growth.

When writers evaluate how they've changed as writers, they acknowledge their feelings and consider how they've grown. When Evan was asked to describe how he changed as a writer from kindergarten to first grade, he wrote, "Last year I was scared. This year [I] am not. Last year I couldn't read my words. Now I can." (See Figure 5.6.)

Evan acknowledged his fear, told what he couldn't do, and explained what he is able to do now. He values being able to read his work.

At the end of his second-grade year, Michael looked back on his portfolio of work. He reflected, "In the first writing I did[,] I did small words and now I do really, really big words. I am so impressed [with] my books now and with my big words. My writing is better. And now I will remember my periods and question marks." (See Figure 5.7.)

Yes, Michael said he values punctuating his work. Yes, Michael forgot to punctuate the last sentence in his reflection. Oh, the irony! But when we look more deeply into Michael's reflection, we learn he has changed. He values the growth of an expanded vocabulary. And he values getting better at his craft.

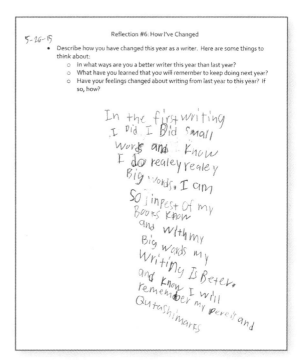

Figure 5.6 Evan's reflection on how he's changed

Figure 5.7 Michael's reflection on how he's changed

Last year I could not
think up any ideas this year
I have too many ideas.
Puncuation is one thing
I will remember for next
year. I used to not
like writing because I
had no ideas.

Figure 5.8 Amber values choice.

Figure 5.9 Helena values the help from her teacher.

Reflection #3: How My Teacher Helped me as a Writer

• Think about your teachers this year and how they helped you as a writer. They might have helped during a lesson, a conference, or an Author's Chair.
  ○ Who helped you?
  ○ How did they help?

When my teachers gave us a
mini lesson, it helped
me understand what
they were teaching us.
My teachers helped alot.

Figure 5.10 Christopher values the help from his teacher.

Amber, a fifth grader, values the change that happened when choice became a value in her classroom (see Figure 5.8). She wrote, "Last year I could not think up any ideas. This year I have too many ideas. Punctuation is one thing I will remember for next year. I used to not like writing because I had no ideas."

Amber recognized her growth as a writer. Last year, when she had no ideas, she didn't like writing. This year, her feelings about writing grew alongside her lists of ideas for writing possibilities.

Writers Value What They Learn From Others.

In a classroom in which the writers drive the workshop, the teacher plays an important role in helping with navigation. And students value the input. I asked Helena, a kindergartner, about her writing—a scene from the movie *Star Wars* (Figure 5.9).

> Brian: Can you tell me what you did today as a writer?
>
> Helena: I did words! I did words!
>
> Brian: Is this something you're excited about?
>
> Helena: Yes! That says "Chewbacca" and that says "Princess Leia." My teacher helped me write it!
>
> Brian: How?
>
> Helena: She helped me with my sounds!

Helena, excited about the gradual addition of print to her drawings, acknowledged the value of having a teacher present to help her with her transition.

Christopher, a fifth grader, reflected on the artifacts he placed in his portfolio. He found a mini-lesson glue-in his teacher gave him about developing characters in writing. He wrote, "When my teachers gave us a mini lesson it helped me understand what they were teaching us. My teachers helped a lot." (See Figure 5.10.)

Writers value what their teachers teach them. Their teachers nudge. And their nudges create stronger products.

When given opportunities to evaluate, to find value in their learning, students reflect the values of the classroom. What does it tell us when students' evaluations say they value choice? Or opportunities to learn from others? Or time in class to simply write? Their evaluations tell us that our values as writing teachers are being reflected in the work of our students. They tell us we are being effective writing teachers.

Travelogue

Teachers create the road conditions for student drivers. They pave the roads that writers use on their journey by clearing barriers. Writers get from one place to the next when they are given *time* to drive. *Choice* allows writers to determine the destination and keeps them excited about the trip. Writers learn how to cruise, slow down, speed up, and take detours when teachers provide *demonstration* and *response*. Writers stay awake, engaged, and safe through comfortable *room structure*. Teachers set high *expectations* and expect students to set high expectations for themselves as they navigate through their writing. And importantly, as writers drive, teachers empower them to *evaluate* every step of their trip—the process, the product, and the reaction of the audience.

Indeed, writers drive the workshop. But skillful teachers clear the way, help navigate, take photographs, and look back on the journey *with* their writers. Conditions help ensure a smooth ride.

Epilogue

*E*arly in the school year, Deb Robson, a second-grade teacher, discovered she had cancer. Frightened, she didn't quite know how to tell her students— or if she should tell them at all. She knew she would miss several days of school. She knew there would be physical changes that her students would notice. But were they too young to handle such serious news?

Deb called a meeting with her students' parents and asked how they would like for her to handle this information with their children. The parents agreed to have an initial conversation with their children but encouraged Deb to talk (and write) about her journey in class as well.

When Deb told her students the news, one little boy—Jacob—raised his hand and spoke. "Ms. Robson," he said, "I've had cancer also."

Deb explained the moment to me this way: "When Jacob announced this to me, Brian, it was so powerful. It was like a spiritual connection. It was as if everything else in the classroom blurred out of vision and all I could see was that little boy telling me, *You are not alone.* He was meant to be in my classroom that year. It's strange. Usually I feel like students need me—but I actually needed him in my classroom that year."

Jacob spent the entire year writing about cancer. Story after story filled his notebooks. He wrote about a stuffed lion he held every time he had chemotherapy. He wrote about his best friend, Jessica, dying in the hospital. He wrote about what it's like to live in a hospital for a year (Figure 6.1). He filled pages and pages with events and

Canser
By Jacob

"Noooooo! Jessica is died." I cried. I felt teribal after she died. Her graet powerful secret love for me will never be replaced. She was my best friend on cancer. I met her in Wolfson Childrens Hospital on level 8. Me and Jessica were in the hospital for four years together. Her canser came back six times. I never will forget Jesecca. It was dredfuly terribly hard on me when I found out she was deid. I knew so much about her. The day before I was frietind for her. Jesecca had dark blond hair. Her eyes shimerd in the sunlit. A leg of hers was raaped up in a shimmering striped pieces of cloth. Jesicca always thought I was the hamsmest kid around all that she did was lae in bed. She didn't have a wheel chair or cruches. She olny had one leg. Whenever I visited her she would ask me if I would like to sit on her leg. We always would talk together. We would always say stuff like "how are you doing, what are you up to latly." She would always listen to what I told and asked her. To my mom she is just a mimery but to me she is still living. It was not that painful on her because she died in her sleep. When I first met her I was scared. I was scared because she only had one leg. When I got to know Jesicca her canser had alwady came back one's. I didn't know that canser could kill us. But when I found out Jesicca died from canser, then I found out canser can kill us.

Figure 6.1 Jacob writes a memoir about his experience with cancer.

experiences that altered his view of the world. Deb read his writing with trepidation—and hope.

The entire year became a journey for both Deb and Jacob. When Deb conferred with Jacob, he told her about his cancer—about his hospital stays, his friends who died, his fear, and his relief of being in remission. He drove the conversation, but Deb gave him suggestions to support him as a writer. She encouraged him to consider a beginning that would hook a reader and an ending that would leave them feeling emotional. She encouraged him to keep writing about a topic that mattered to him. When writers drive the workshop, the conference is a conversation that teaches both the teacher and the student.

When Jacob sat in the author's chair, he would read his writing to friends and ask them if they had questions. They wanted to know more about how it felt to have cancer—if it hurt or if it was scary. His peers asked good questions—questions for him to consider when revising. Deb reiterated to Jacob the importance of these questions. "Readers want to know what this experience felt like for you, so it might be a good writing move to add those feelings to your piece." Jacob did. When writers drive the workshop, they guide the response they need from their peers and teachers.

Jacob reflected on what made a difference to him as a writer. "We write every day for about an hour," he said. Jacob knows that the time he spent every day honing his craft made him a stronger writer. When writers drive the workshop, reflecting on their learning allows them to see what makes a difference in their writing lives.

Often, the writing Jacob placed on his page inspired mini-lessons for Deb to explore with all the children in her classroom. When she saw Jacob use a powerful phrase, it became an opportunity to teach her students how to make their writing resonate with voice. When she noticed that Jacob struggled with beginnings, she conferred with several other students and discovered it was a pattern among most of them. Again, she crafted lessons based on what she saw from her writers. When writers drive the workshop, mini-lessons aren't prescribed—they emerge from the work of the writers.

Jacob blossomed as a writer because Deb created the conditions in the classroom that would cultivate and sustain him. She gave him time every day to work on his craft. She allowed him to choose his writing topics because she knew he needed to write about the cancer that changed his life. She conferred with him often and gave him the response he needed to maintain energy and push forward. And in the process of responding, she learned a lot herself. When writers drive the workshop, the conditions teachers establish in the classroom determine whether the drive will be a smooth or a bumpy one.

Jacob was in Deb's classroom sixteen years ago. I got in touch with Jacob and Deb all these years later to get his permission to use his writing in this book. Thankfully, his cancer never came back. He is now a healthy man in his twenties finding his way through a life that gave him a second chance. Deb is also healthy—still teaching, still inspiring, and still empowering her students to made bold choices and write with strong voices. She's still making a difference in the lives of her students. And they are still making a difference in her life as well. This is what happens when we allow students to drive the workshop.

Appendix

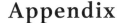

Chapter 1

Questions to Ask for Goals-Oriented Conferences

At the beginning of a genre study:

- What do you hope to learn during this genre study?
- What do you want to accomplish during this genre study?
- When do you want to accomplish this?
- What do you want to do to get better as a writer?
- What have you learned that you want to continue doing this time?
- How are you going to go about accomplishing this writing goal?

In the middle of a genre study:

- How are you doing on your goals so far?
- Are you accomplishing what you set out to do?
- Do you think you'll have this goal accomplished by the end of the study?

At the end of a genre study:

- Did you meet your goal?
- In what ways did you meet or not meet your goal?
- What do you know now that you didn't know before starting this study?
- What goals do you think you'll set for yourself for the next study?

Questions to Ask for Process Conferences

Planning Questions	Drafting Questions	Revision Questions
• Can you tell me about your [genre] idea? • Can you tell me why you like this topic? • Do you need to interview? Observe? Read? • Would you like to talk to a classmate? • Do you need to change your topic? • Tell me all you know about this topic. • Can you find pictures or photographs that will help? • Have you thought about the ending? • Retell and jot down the main parts of your story. • Where do you want to begin? • What details from your list or ideas do you want to include? • What do you want your piece to say? • How would you like to record your plan?	• Reread your ideas and plan. • Do you know the topic well enough to write about it? • Why are you writing this piece? (purpose) • What do you hope to do with this piece of writing? (reason for writing) • Who is your audience, and what do they need to know to enjoy this? • What must you include to satisfy your audience? • What information can you remove and save for another piece? • Do you need to collect more ideas? • What are you trying to say to others?	• Access all the revision lessons you've taught. Use this advice to guide the writer's revisions. • Have you included all the criteria we talked about in class? • What's your best part? Can you make other parts that good? Do you have too few details? Too many? • Are you saying more than one thing in this piece? • What's the one thing you're trying to say? • Have you tried writing other leads? • Does the ending make sense? • Can you combine sentences so the piece flows? • Are the characters well developed? • Is the story problem sensible? • Did you use strong verbs? • Did you use strong nouns? • Do you repeat yourself? • Are the settings clear to your audience? • Do you need dialogue? • Is the dialogue realistic? Believable? • Are the parts in logical order? • Does the ending/conclusion leave a reader satisfied?

Questions to Ask for Genre/Skills Conferences: Kindergarten

Opinion Writing	Informational Writing	Narrative Writing
• **Purpose:** Why are you writing this opinion piece?	• **Purpose:** Why are you writing this informational piece?	• **Purpose:** Why are you writing this story?
• **Audience:** Who are you writing this for?	• **Audience:** Who are you writing this for?	• **Audience:** Who are you writing this for?
• Structure Questions □ **Overall:** Did you tell me your opinion (or likes/dislikes) about this topic? □ **Lead:** Let's talk about how you could begin this piece with your opinion. □ **Transitions:** Let's see if you can add some more.... (using words like *because*) □ **Ending:** Tell me how you ended this piece of writing. □ **Organization:** Did you tell, draw, write your opinion in one place and in another place say why?	• Structure Questions □ **Overall:** Tell me what you're writing today. □ **Lead:** Did you tell us what you're writing about on the first page? □ **Transitions:** Did you put different things you know about this topic on each page? □ **Ending:** Tell me how you ended this piece of writing. □ **Organization:** Did you write, tell, draw information across several pages?	• Structure Questions □ **Overall:** Tell me about your whole story. □ **Lead:** Did you tell us what happened first? □ **Transitions:** Are your pages in order? What's missing? What needs to be rearranged? □ **Ending:** Tell me how you ended your story. □ **Organization:** Did you have a page for your beginning, a page for your middle, and a page for your ending?
• Development Questions □ **Elaboration:** What else could you say about this topic? □ **Craft:** Could you add more details in your pictures/words?	• Development Questions □ **Elaboration:** What else could you say/draw/write about this topic? □ **Craft:** Could you add more details in your pictures/words?	• Development Questions □ **Elaboration:** Did your story tell about who was there, what they did, and how the characters felt? □ **Craft:** Could you add more details in your pictures/words?

Questions to Ask for Genre/Skills Conferences: First Grade

Opinion Writing	Informational Writing	Narrative Writing
• **Purpose:** Why are you writing this opinion piece?	• **Purpose:** Why are you writing this informational piece?	• **Purpose:** Why are you writing this story?
• **Audience:** Who are you writing this for?	• **Audience:** Who are you writing this for?	• **Audience:** Who are you writing this for?
• **Structure Questions** □ **Overall:** Did you write your opinion (or likes/dislikes) and say why? □ **Lead:** Did you write your opinion in the beginning? Did you get the reader's attention? Did you name the topic? □ **Transitions:** Did you add words such as *and* and *because*? □ **Ending:** Tell me how you ended this piece of writing. □ **Organization:** Did you write a part where you got the reader's attention and a part where you said more?	• **Structure Questions** □ **Overall:** What are you telling readers about with your informational piece? □ **Lead:** Did you name your topic in the beginning and get the reader's attention? □ **Transitions:** Did you tell about different parts of your topic on different pages? □ **Ending:** Did you write an ending? □ **Organization:** Did you tell about a topic part by part?	• **Structure Questions** □ **Overall:** Tell me about your story. □ **Lead:** Did you try a beginning for your story? □ **Transitions:** Did you put your pages in order? Did you use words like *such as, and then,* and *so*? □ **Ending:** Did you find a way to end your story? □ **Organization:** Is your story three or more pages long?
• **Development Questions** □ **Elaboration:** Did you write at least one reason for your opinion? □ **Craft:** Did you use labels and words to give details?	• **Development Questions** □ **Elaboration:** Did you put facts in your writing to teach us about the topic? □ **Craft:** Did you use labels and words to give facts?	• **Development Questions** □ **Elaboration:** Is the picture that you saw in your mind what you put on the page? Did you add details in the pictures and the words? □ **Craft:** Did you use labels and words to give more details?

When Writers Drive the Workshop by Brian Kissel

Questions to Ask for Genre/Skills Conferences: Second Grade

Opinion Writing	Informational Writing	Narrative Writing
• **Purpose:** Why are you writing this opinion piece?	• **Purpose:** Why are you writing this informational piece?	• **Purpose:** Why are you writing this story?
• **Audience:** Who are you writing this for?	• **Audience:** Who are you writing this for?	• **Audience:** Who are you writing this for?

• Structure Questions
  □ **Overall:** Did you write your opinion (or likes/dislikes) and give reasons?
  □ **Lead:** Did you write your opinion in the beginning? Did you get the reader's attention? Did you write in a way that tried to convince your reader of your opinion?
  □ **Transitions:** Did you add words such as *also, another,* and *because*?
  □ **Ending:** Did you end your piece in a way that reminded your readers of your opinion?
  □ **Organization:** Did you write different parts? Did you write several lines for each part?
	• Structure Questions
	  □ **Overall:** Did you teach readers about your topic and include important points?
	  □ **Lead:** Did you write a beginning that names your subject? Did you write a beginning that makes readers want to read it further?
	  □ **Transitions:** Did you use words like *and* and *also* to show that you had more to say?
	  □ **Ending:** Did you write some sentences or a section to end your informational piece?
	  □ **Organization:** Did your writing have different parts? Did each part tell different information about a topic?
		• Structure Questions
		  □ **Overall:** Tell me about your story.
		  □ **Lead:** Does your story have a good beginning? Did you choose to begin it with an action, some talk, or a setting that makes it interesting to read?
		  □ **Transitions:** Did you tell your story in some sort of order using words like *when, then,* and *after*?
		  □ **Ending:** Did you end your story with an action, talk, or some kind of feeling?
		  □ **Organization:** Did you write a lot of lines on a page and write across several pages?

• Development Questions
  □ **Elaboration:** Did you write at least two reasons and write a few sentences about each one?
  □ **Craft:** Did you choose words that would make readers agree with your opinion?
	• Development Questions
	  □ **Elaboration:** Did you use different kinds of information in your writing such as facts, definitions, details, steps, and tips?
	  □ **Craft:** Did you include words that show you are an expert on this topic?
		• Development Questions
		  □ **Elaboration:** Did you try to bring your characters to life with details, talk, and actions?
		  □ **Craft:** Did you choose strong words that help readers picture your story?

Questions to Ask for Genre/Skills Conferences: Third Grade

Opinion Writing	Informational Writing	Narrative Writing
• **Purpose:** Why are you writing this opinion piece?	• **Purpose:** Why are you writing this informational piece?	• **Purpose:** Why are you writing this story?
• **Audience:** Who are you writing this for?	• **Audience:** Who are you writing this for?	• **Audience:** Who are you writing this for?
• Structure Questions	• Structure Questions	• Structure Questions
□ **Overall:** Did you tell your readers your opinion and ideas on a topic and help them understand your reasons?	□ **Overall:** Did you teach readers information about your subject? Did you put in ideas, observations, and questions?	□ **Overall:** Tell me about your whole story.
□ **Lead:** Did you set your readers up in the beginning to know what to expect? Did you hook them into caring about your opinion?	□ **Lead:** Did you tell us what you're writing about on the first page? Did you get us ready for the information we are about to learn?	□ **Lead:** Did you write a beginning that helps readers know about the characters? Did you include a setting in your story?
□ **Transitions:** Did you connect ideas and reasons by using words like *for example* and *because*? Did you connect one reason or example using words like *also* and *another*?	□ **Transitions:** Did you put different words to show sequence like *before, after, then,* and *later*? Did you use words to show what did not fit such as *however* and *but*?	□ **Transitions:** Did you tell your story in order? Did you use phrases such as *a little later* and *after that*?
□ **Ending:** Did you end your piece with a thought or a comment related to your opinion?	□ **Ending:** Did you write an ending that drew conclusions, asked questions, or suggested ways readers might respond?	□ **Ending:** Do you end your story with an action, talk, or feeling? Did you work hard to end the story in an interesting way?
□ **Organization:** Did you write several reasons or examples why readers should agree with your opinion? Did you write several sentences about each reason? Was your writing mostly about one thing?	□ **Organization:** Did you group your information into different parts? Was each part mostly about one thing that connected to your big topic?	□ **Organization:** Did you use paragraphs? Do you start each new part with a new paragraph?

When Writers Drive the Workshop by Brian Kissel   Copyright © 2017. Stenhouse Publishers.

Questions to Ask for Genre/Skills Conferences: Third Grade (continued)

Opinion Writing	Informational Writing	Narrative Writing

• Development Questions
    □ **Elaboration:** Did you name your reasons to support your opinion? Did you write more about each opinion?
    □ **Craft:** Did you tell your readers to believe you? Did you write in ways that got readers thinking or feeling in a certain way?
	• Development Questions
	    □ **Elaboration:** Did you write facts, definitions, details, and observations about your topic and explain some of them?
	    □ **Craft:** Did you choose expert words to teach readers a lot about the subject? As a writer, did you teach readers a lot about the subject? Did the way you present the information interest readers? Did you use drawings, captions, or diagrams?
		• Development Questions
		    □ **Elaboration:** Do you show what happened to your characters? Do you show different ways that reveal what your character(s) think?
		    □ **Craft:** Did you write a story in a way that got readers to picture what happened? Did you bring your story to life?

Questions to Ask for Genre/Skills Conferences: Fourth Grade

Opinion Writing	Informational Writing	Narrative Writing
• **Purpose:** Why are you writing this opinion piece?	• **Purpose:** Why are you writing this informational piece?	• **Purpose:** Why are you writing this story?
• **Audience:** Who are you writing this for?	• **Audience:** Who are you writing this for?	• **Audience:** Who are you writing this for?
• Structure Questions	• Structure Questions	• Structure Questions
□ **Overall:** Did you make a claim about a topic and support it with reasons?	□ **Overall:** Did you teach readers information about your subject? Did you put facts, details, quotes, and ideas into each part of your piece?	□ **Overall:** Tell me about your story? Do you think you told it in a way that will entertain readers?
□ **Lead:** Did you hook your readers? Did you explain why the topic mattered, or ask a question, giving a surprising fact, or give background information? Did you state your claim?	□ **Lead:** Did you hook your readers by telling why your topic matters, telling a surprising fact, or giving a big picture? Did you let readers know what you would teach them in this writing?	□ **Lead:** Did you write a beginning that showed what happened and where?
□ **Transitions:** Did you connect ideas and reasons by using words like *for example, another example, one time and for instance?* Did you shift from saying reasons to giving evidence using words like *in addition to, also,* and another to show that you wanted to make a new point?	□ **Transitions:** Did you put different words to show how one piece of information connects with others? Words like *before, later, next, then,* and *after?* Did you organize sections in parts by using words like *another, also,* and *for example?*	□ **Transitions:** Did you show how much time went by in your story by marking time with words/phrases like *just then, suddenly, after a while,* and *a little later?*
□ **Ending:** Did restate your opinion? Or did you reflect on your claim suggesting an action or response based on what you wrote?	□ **Ending:** Did your ending remind readers of your subject? Did the ending have a follow-up action or leave readers with a final insight? Did you add thoughts, feelings, and questions about the subject at the end?	□ **Ending:** Does your ending make sense? Is it connected to what you wrote at the beginning and middle parts? Did you use action, dialogue, or feelings to bring your story to a close?
□ **Organization:** Did you separate sections of your information using paragraphs?	□ **Organization:** Did you group the information into sections and use paragraphs and chapters to separate those sections? Did you use headings or subheadings?	□ **Organization:** Did you use paragraphs to separate different parts or times of your story? Did you show when new characters were speaking?

When Writers Drive the Workshop by Brian Kissel

Questions to Ask for Genre/Skills Conferences: Fourth Grade (continued)

Opinion Writing	Informational Writing	Narrative Writing
• Development Questions 　□ **Elaboration:** Did you give reasons to support your opinion? Did you choose reasons to convince your readers? Did you include examples and information to support your reasons—perhaps from a text, your knowledge, or from your life? 　□ **Craft:** Did you make deliberate words choices to convince readers (repeating words or emphasizing words that struck at a reader's emotions)? Did you choose precise details and facts? Did you choose the best evidence to support your points? Did you have a convincing tone?	• Development Questions 　□ **Elaboration:** Did you teach readers different things about your subject? Did you choose subtopics because they were important and interesting? Did you include different kinds of facts and details such as numbers, names, and examples? Did you get information from talking to people, reading books, and from your own knowledge and observations? Did you make compare/contrast, use cause/effect, pro/con? Did you use diagrams, charts, headings, bold words, definition boxes to help readers? 　□ **Craft:** Did you make deliberate word choices by repeating key words? Did you choose interesting comparisons and figurative language to clarify points? Did you make choices about what is best to include/not include? Did you use a teaching tone?	• Development Questions 　□ **Elaboration:** Did you add more to the heart (or most important part) of your story? Did you include actions? Dialogue? Thoughts and feelings? 　□ **Craft:** Did you show why characters did what they did by including their thinking? Did you make some parts of the story go quickly? Did you slow some parts (the important ones) down? Did you use precise words, sensory details, and/or figurative language to make your story come to life? Did you use a storytelling voice? Did you convey emotion? Did you use descriptions, phrases, dialogue, and thoughts?

Questions to Ask for Genre/Skills Conferences: Fifth Grade

Opinion Writing	Informational Writing	Narrative Writing
• **Purpose:** Why are you writing this opinion piece?	• **Purpose:** Why are you writing this informational piece?	• **Purpose:** Why are you writing this story?
• **Audience:** Who are you writing this for?	• **Audience:** Who are you writing this for?	• **Audience:** Who are you writing this for?
• Structure Questions	• Structure Questions	• Structure Questions
□ **Overall:** Did you make a claim or thesis about a topic and support it with reasons? Did you provide a variety of evidence for each reason?	□ **Overall:** Did you teach readers information about your subject? Did you include little essays, stories, or how-to sections in your writing?	□ **Overall:** Tell me about your story? Is it something that really happened?
□ **Lead:** Did you write an introduction that led to the claim? Do you think your readers care about your opinion? Did you tell what is significant about your opinion?	□ **Lead:** Did you hook your readers by getting them interested in your topic? Did you let readers know the subtopics that you will develop later?	□ **Lead:** Did you write a beginning that showed what happened and where? Did you give some clues about the problem that would happen to the main character?
□ **Transitions:** Did you use transition words in different ways: To connect evidence and reasons (*this shows that*), to help readers follow thinking (*another reason, the most important reason*), to show what happened (*consequently and because of*), to be more precise (*specifically and in particular*)?	□ **Transitions:** When you wrote about results, did you use words and phrases like *consequently, as a result,* and *because of this*? When you compared information, did you use phrases such as *in contrast, by comparison,* and *especially*? In narrative parts, did you use phrases like *a little later*? In opinion parts did you use phrases like *most important reason, for example,* and *consequently*?	□ **Transitions:** Did you show the passage of time by describing things happening at the same time (*meanwhile, at the same time*) or flashback and flash forward (*early that morning, three hours later*)?
□ **Ending:** Did your ending connect back to what the text was mainly about?	□ **Ending:** Did you write a conclusion that restated the main points? Did you offer a final thought or question for readers to consider?	□ **Ending:** Does your ending make sense? Is it connected to what you wrote at the beginning and middle? Did your character realize something at the end of the story that came from the events that happened earlier? Does the reader have closure?
□ **Organization:** Did you group information into related ideas/paragraphs? Is your writing in an order that helps prove reasons and claims?	□ **Organization:** Did you organize your writing into a sequence of separate sections? Did you use headings and subheadings to highlight separate sections? Did you write each section according to an organizational plan?	□ **Organization:** Did you use paragraphs to separate different parts or times of your story? Did you show when new characters were speaking? Were some parts of the story longer and more developed than others?

When Writers Drive the Workshop by Brian Kissel   Copyright © 2017. Stenhouse Publishers.

Questions to Ask for Genre/Skills Conferences: Fifth Grade (continued)

Opinion Writing	Informational Writing	Narrative Writing

• Development Questions
  □ **Elaboration:** Did you give reasons to support your opinion that didn't overlap with other reasons? Did you put them in a convincing order? Did you include evidence such as facts, examples, quotes, micro-stories, and information to support claims? Did you discuss evidence that went with the claim?
  □ **Craft:** Did you make deliberate words choices to convince readers (repeating words or emphasizing words that struck at a reader's emotions)? Did you choose precise words and phrases to support your points? Did you use a scholarly voice to vary sentences?
	• Development Questions
	  □ **Elaboration:** Did you explain different aspects of the subject? Did you include a variety of information such as examples, details, dates, and quotes? Did you use trusted sources and give credit when appropriate? Did you work to make this information understandable to readers? Did you summarize background information? Did you let readers know when you were stating facts and when you were offering your own thinking?
	  □ **Craft:** Did you make deliberate word choices by using vocabulary of experts and explaining key terms? Did you use exact phrases, comparisons, or images to explain information and concepts? Did you make choices about how to teach the information (e.g., storytelling, summary, and other genre features)? Did you use a consistent teaching tone?
		• Development Questions
		  □ **Elaboration:** Did you develop realistic characters? Did you develop the details, actions, dialogue, and internal thinking that contributed to the deeper meaning of the story?
		  □ **Craft:** Did you show why characters did what they did by including their thinking and responses to what happened? Did you make some parts of the story go quickly (less important parts)? Did you slow some parts (the important ones) down? Did you use precise words, sensory details, and/or figurative language to make your story come to life? Did you use a storytelling voice? Did you convey emotion? Did you use descriptions, phrases, dialogue, and thoughts? Did you use symbols to bring forth meaning? Did you vary sentences to change pace and tone?

Questions to Ask for Publication and Portfolio Conferences

Publication Questions	Portfolio Questions
• How do you think you'll publish this piece? • What materials do you need in order to publish this piece the way you want it to be published? • Is there an author you want to use as a mentor for your published piece? • How long do you think it will take you to publish this? • What are some ways you can publish this so that it's engaging for readers?	• Which piece did you choose to include in your portfolio? Why did you choose this piece? • What does this piece say about you as a writer? • What does this piece show about you as a learner? • How do you think others will react to this piece of writing? • By looking across your portfolio pieces, how do you think you've grown as a writer? • What do you now know as a writer that you didn't know last year? • After learning what you've learned, what do you think you could teach others to do as a writer?

Conferring Sheet

Name: _____

Date						
Genre						
Type of Conference						
What We Discussed						
Strengths						
Challenges						
Possible Mini-Lessons						

Chapter 2

Tips for Generating Ideas for Narrative Writing

Generating Ideas for Writing
Mini-Lessons

Narrative Writing (Memoirs, Personal Narrative, Stories, Poetry)

Three Meaningful Objects

- Students bring three objects from home.
- Share their objects with a small group.
- Describe one of their objects aloud with the whole class.
- The whole class makes connections to the object and writes a list of different ideas.
- Student either writes about one of the objects OR writes about something inspired by someone else's object.

Life Time Lines

- Draw a line across the middle of your daybook.
- Think of different events that happened in your life.
- Write the positive experiences above the line.
- Write the negative experiences below the line.
- Circle three experiences.
- Pick one experience and write about it for three minutes. Pick a second experience and write about it for two minutes. Pick a third experience and write about it for one minute.
- Decide: Which experience do I want to explore more deeply today as a writer?

Tips for Generating Ideas for Narrative Writing (continued)

Home Places

- Draw a picture of where you live or a place that is meaningful to you (e.g., home, apartment, grandma's house, place of worship).
- Draw pictures of scenes that took place inside this place.
- Draw pictures of scenes that took place outside this place.
- Use one of those drawings to start a draft.

People, Places, Things

- In your daybook draw three columns and write these headings: People, Places, Things
- In column one: Think of people from your life who have influenced you (both good and bad). Make a list of these people.
- In column two: Think of all the different places in your life that hold meaning (both good and bad). Make a list of these places.
- In column three: Think of all the different things you know something about (how to cook, how to play a sport, cancer, friendship, video games, etc.). Make a list of these things.
- Pick one thing from your list and draft. This may be a piece of fiction, a memoir, a poem, a non fiction piece, a persuasive essay, an informational text, etc.

Tips for Generating Ideas for Persuasive Writing

Generating Ideas for Persuasive Writing
Mini-Lessons

Generating Ideas for Writing–Global Audiences

- If you could change the world with your writing, what would you want to change about the world?
- Brainstorm a list of different causes that you feel passionate about and make a chart that includes the following:

Important Cause	Who Do I Want to Inform?	What Do I Hope to Accomplish Through My Writing?

Generating Topics for Persuasive Writing–Local Audiences

- What things would you change about school?
- Brainstorm a list of different things you want to change about school. Who do you need to convince to make those changes?
- Think about a way you might be able to persuade them to make that change.

What I would change about school...	Who can make that change happen?	How might I convince that person to make the change?

Tips for Generating Ideas for Informational Writing

Generating Ideas for Informational Writing
Mini-Lessons

Brainstorming Purposes and Audiences for Informational Writing

- Bring in a variety of informational texts (reports, newspaper clippings, sports pages, advice columns, instructional manuals, cookbooks, etc.)
- What kind of information do we see every day in our lives? What is the purpose of this writing? Who does it teach?

Type of Informational Text	Purpose of the Text	Audience

Brainstorming Topics for All About Writing

- With your class, engage in a brainstorming session about All About Books. Chart responses so students get multiple ideas.

What is something you already know a lot about?	What is something you want to know more about?	Who could you teach with your writing?

- Together, as a class, brainstorm different topics and ways to publish those topics. For example, students might want to write a research report about skateboarding. They can publish something about this topic by *describing* it within a multigenre book, *explaining* about it in an interactive demonstration, *instructing* how to skateboard by writing a manual or creating a rule book, or *retelling information* by writing about other important skateboarding figures.

Mini-Lesson Daybook Sheet: The Author Speaks

Author's Chair: The Author Speaks!

How do we speak when we are sharing in the chair?

- Loudly!

- Boldly!

- Confidently!

Tell us how you want us to respond.

- Questions, Compliments, Suggestions, Connections, Ideas

Mini-Lesson Daybook Sheet: The Audience Responds

Author's Chair: The Audience Responds

How do we show the author respect when they are sharing in the Author's Chair?

- We listen the way the author wants us to listen.

- We look at the author.

- We don't distract.

- We quiet down and stop talking with friends.

- We listen for ways we can support the author.

- We give response that helps (not hurts) the author.

- We think: What can I say that might help this author?

- Before we speak we ask ourselves: How can I say this to the author in a respectful way?

Author's Chair
Teacher Documentation

Author/Date	Type of Response Sought	What I Noticed	Instructional Implications

When Writers Drive the Workshop by Brian Kissel   Copyright © 2017. Stenhouse Publishers.

Chapter 3

Daybook Sheet of Reflection Questions

Reflection Questions

Looking Back Questions

- What did you end up doing as a writer today?
- Looking back, how did you spend your time today as a writer?
- What struggles did you have today as a writer?
- What successes did you have today as a writer?
- Looking back across your year so far, what have you noticed about yourself as a writer?
- Who helped you today? How did that person help?

Looking Forward Questions

- In the future, in what ways do you hope to improve as a writer?
- What's one thing you want to improve in the piece of writing you worked on today?
- Tomorrow, when you start writing again, what's one thing you are going to change about your piece?
- In what ways do you want to change as a writer?
- What are your plans for the rest of this genre study?
- What are your strengths as a writer that you plan to carry forward into future pieces of writing?
- What's one thing you have seen from your peers that you would like to try in future pieces of writing?
- What's a goal you would like to set for yourself next time?

Daybook Sheet of Reflection Questions (continued)

Looking Inward Questions

- How do you feel about the work you did today as a writer? What did you like? Dislike? Why?
- How did writing make you feel today? Think about drawing a picture of your face and using one word to describe this.
- How did you feel about your process today?
- Did you learn anything new about yourself as a writer today? If so, what?
- Did you learn anything new about yourself as a person from writing today? If so, what?
- What does your writing topic reveal about you as a writer?
- How are you changing as a writer this year?

Looking Outward Questions

- Who has influenced you as a writer?
- How do you think your writing is different from the way other people write?
- If you were the teacher, what would you write on a sticky note and leave on your piece of writing?
- What is a word (or phrase or line or section or paragraph) you think others will really notice when they read this piece of writing?
- When you look at your self-assessment, in what ways are you meeting the standards listed?
- When you look at your self-assessment, in what ways do you think you should improve your writing?
- In what ways have mentor authors supported you as a writer?

WRITE Goals Sheet

Name: _____ Date: _____ Genre Unit of Study: _____

WRITE Goals

Writing Your Goal(s) • Name your goal(s).	
Reaching Your Goal(s) • Describe how you will reach your goal(s).	
Involving Others in Your Goals • Name others who might help you achieve your goal(s). • Describe how they might help.	
Timing Your Goals • Set a date for when you intend to achieve this goal.	
Evaluating Your Goals • Describe what it looks like when you successfully achieve your goal.	

Chapter 4

Studying Conference Notes

Previous Genre Study: _____

	Students were *successful* with this during the previous genre study	Students *struggled* with this during the previous genre study
Process		
Skills		

Studying Author's Chair Notes

Author's Chair Analysis

Time Period: From _____ to _____

Types of Response	How Do Peers Respond?
Who Offered Feedback?	**Who Didn't Offer Feedback?**
What Is the Quality of the Feedback?	**Possible Mini-Lessons to Teach**

Studying Reflection Notes

Type of Reflection	What I See in Students' Reflections	Possible Socratic Seminar Questions
Quick-write questions focused on looking back		
Goals sheets		
Portfolios		

Studying Mentor Authors

Mentor Authors

Craft Focus: _____

Text/Author	Direct from the Text	Recommended to Use for a Whole-Class Mini-Lesson	
		Yes	No
		Yes	No
		Yes	No
		Yes	No
		Yes	No
		Yes	No
		Yes	No

References

Anderson, Carl. 2000. *How's It Going? A Practical Guide to Conferring with Student Writers.* Portsmouth, NH: Heinemann.

Anderson, Jeff. 2005. *Mechanically Inclined: Building Grammar, Usage, and Style into Writer's Workshop.* Portland, ME: Stenhouse.

_____ . 2007. *Everyday Editing: Inviting Students to Develop Skill and Craft in Writer's Workshop.* Portland, ME: Stenhouse.

Atwell, Nancie. 1998. *In the Middle: New Understandings About Writing, Reading, and Learning.* Portsmouth, NH: Heinemann.

Brannon, Lillian, Sally Griffin, Karen Haag, Anthony Iannone, Cynthia Urbanski, and Shana Woodward. 2008. *Thinking Out Loud on Paper: The Student Daybook as a Tool to Foster Learning.* Portsmouth, NH: Heinemann.

Bridge, Connie, and Elfrieda Heibert. 1985. "A Comparison of Classroom Writing Practices, Teachers' Perceptions of Their Writing Instruction, and Textbook Recommendations on Writing Practices." *Elementary School Journal* 86: 155–172.

Buckner, Aimee. 2005. *Notebook Know-How: Strategies for the Writer's Notebook.* Portland, ME: Stenhouse.

_____ . 2013. *Nonfiction Notebooks: Strategies for Informational Writing.* Portland, ME: Stenhouse.

Calkins, Lucy. 1994. *The Art of Teaching Writing.* Portsmouth, NH: Heinemann.

Csikszentmihalyi, Mihaly. 1990. *Flow: The Psychology of Optimal Experience*. New York: Harper and Row.

Draper, Mary, Mary Alice Barksdale-Ladd, and Marguerite Radencich. 2000. "Reading and Writing Habits of Preservice Teachers." *Reading Horizons* 40 (3): 187–203.

Dweck, Carol. 2007. *Mindset: How You Can Fulfill Your Potential*. London: Constable and Robinson.

Faery, Rebecca. 1993. "Teachers and Writers: The Faculty Writer's Workshop and Writing Across the Curriculum." *WPA: Writing Program Administration* 17: 31–42.

Fletcher, Ralph. 2006. *Boy Writers: Reclaiming Their Voices*. Portland, ME: Stenhouse.

Fletcher, Ralph, and JoAnn Portalupi. 2001. *Writer's Workshop: The Essential Guide*. Portsmouth, NH: Heinemann.

_____ . 2007. *Craft Lessons: Teaching Writing K–8*. 2nd ed. Portland, ME: Stenhouse.

Graves, Donald. (1983) 2003. *Writing: Teachers and Children at Work*. Portsmouth, NH: Heinemann.

_____ . 1994. *A Fresh Look at Writing*. Portsmouth, NH: Heinemann.

_____ . 2004. *Teaching Day by Day*. Portsmouth, NH: Heinemann.

Graves, Donald, and Jane Hansen. 1983. "The Author's Chair." *Language Arts* 60: 176–183.

Hansen, Jane. (1985) 2005. *When Writers Read*. Portsmouth, NH: Heinemann.

_____ . 1998. *When Learners Evaluate*. Portsmouth, NH: Heinemann.

Hollingsworth, Sandra. 1988. "Making Field-Based Programs Work: A Three-Level Approach to Reading Instruction." *Journal of Teacher Education* 33: 28–36.

Johnston, Peter. 2004. *Choice Words: How Our Language Affects Children's Learning*. Portland, ME: Stenhouse.

_____ . 2012. *Opening Minds: Using Language to Change Lives*. Portland, ME: Stenhouse.

Kissel, Brian, and Erin Miller. 2015. "Reclaiming Power in the Writer's Workshop: Defending Curricula, Countering Narratives, and Changing Identities in Pre-Kindergarten Classrooms." *The Reading Teacher* 69 (1): 77–86.

Kissel, Brian, Erin Miller, and Jane Hansen. 2013. "What's New About Writers' Workshop: Using Retro Ideas to Re-envision Student Led Agendas." In *What's New in Literacy Teaching? Weaving Together Time-Honored Practices with New*

Research ed. Karen Wood, Jeanne Paratore, Brian Kissel, and Rachel McCormack. Newark, DE: International Literacy Association.

Kissel, Brian, Katie Stover, and Crystal Glover. 2014. "Bringing Lives into Literacy: Teachers Learn About Choice, Audience, and Response Through Multigenre Writing." *Reading Matters* 14: 41–45.

Lamott, Anne. 2010. "Time Lost and Found." Retrieved from http://www.sunset.com/ travel/anne-lamott-how-to-find-time.

Maslow, Abraham, Robert Frager, and Ruth Cox. 1970. *Motivation and Personality.* Vol. 2, ed. James Fadiman and Cynthia McReynolds. New York: Harper and Row.

McCallister, Cynthia. 2008. "The Author's Chair Revisited." *Curriculum Inquiry* 38 (4): 455–471.

McCarthey, Sarah. 2008. "The Impact of No Child Left Behind on Teachers' Writing Instruction." *Written Communication* 25 (4): 462–505.

Miller, Debbie, Photopia Productions, and Stenhouse Publishers. 2002. *Happy Reading! Creating a Predictable Structure for Joyful Teaching and Learning.* Portland, ME: Stenhouse.

Murray, Donald. 2004. *A Writer Teaches Writing.* 2nd ed. Boston: Thomas/Heinle.

National Council of Teachers of English (NCTE). 2009. *Standards for the Assessment of Reading and Writing.* Rev. ed. http://www.ncte.org/standards/ assessmentstandards.

Ray, Katie Wood. 2006. *Study Driven: A Framework for Planning Units of Study in the Writing Workshop.* Portsmouth, NH: Heinemann.

Ray, Katie Wood, and Lester Laminack. 2001. *The Writer's Workshop: Working Through the Hard Parts (and They're All Hard Parts).* Urbana, IL: National Council of Teachers of English.

Routman, Regie. 2004. *Writing Essentials: Raising Expectations and Results While Simplifying Teaching.* Portsmouth, NH: Heinemann.

Yancy, Kathleen. 1998. *Reflection in the Writing Classroom.* Logan: Utah State University Press.

Yeager, David, and Carol Dweck. 2012. "Mindsets That Promote Resilience: When Students Believe That Personal Characteristics Can Be Developed." *Educational Psychologist* 47 (4): 302–314.

Children's Literature Cited

Howard, Elizabeth Fitzgerald, and James Ransome. 1995. *Aunt Flossie's Hats (and Crab Cakes Later).* New York: HMH Books for Young Readers.

Igus, Toyomi, and Daryl Wells. 2001. *Two Mrs. Gibsons.* New York: Lee and Low Books.

Rylant, Cynthia, and Diane Goode. 1993. *When I Was Young in the Mountains.* New York: Puffin Books.

Willems, Mo, and Jon Scieszka. 2004. *Don't Let the Pigeon Drive the Bus!* London: Walker Books.

Index